WORT FÜR WORT

New Advanced Vocabulary

PAUL STOCKER

HODDER
EDUCATION
PART OF HACHETTE LIVRE UK

Acknowledgements

I should like to thank Evelyn Schmitz and Martin Fries for their invaluable help in preparing this book, and their many useful suggestions.

Although every effort has been made to ensure that website addresses are correct at time of going to press, Hodder Murray cannot be held responsible for the content of any website mentioned in this book. It is sometimes possible to find a relocated web page by typing in the address of the home page for a website in the URL window of your browser.

Hodder Headline's policy is to use papers that are natural, renewable and recyclable products and made from wood grown in sustainable forests. The logging and manufacturing processes are expected to conform to the environmental regulations of the country of origin.

Orders: please contact Bookpoint Ltd, 130 Milton Park, Abingdon, Oxon OX14 4SB. Telephone: (44) 01235 827720. Fax: (44) 01235 400454. Lines are open 9.00–5.00, Monday to Saturday, with a 24-hour message answering service. Visit our website at www.hoddereducation.co.uk

© Paul Stocker
First published in 1992
Second edition 1996
Third edition 2000
This fourth edition published 2006 by
Hodder Education, part of Hachette Livre UK
338 Euston Road
London NW1 3BH

Impression number 10 9 8 7 6 5 4
Year   2010 2009 2008

Cover photo © Robert Harding/Digital Vision/Getty Images
Typeset by Transet Limited, Coventry, England.
Printed in Great Britain for Hodder Education, part of Hachette Livre UK, 338 Euston Road, London NW1 3BH, by
Cox & Wyman Ltd, Reading, Berkshire.

A catalogue record for this title is available from the British Library

ISBN 978 0340 915 226

Introduction

This new edition is fully up-dated with material taken from books and all types of media. Each unit is organised as follows:

- Basic words in a shaded box. In a few units there are several of these boxes.

- A number of sub-sections on aspects of the main topic. Each starts with a list of single vocabulary items in alphabetical order, and finishes with longer phrases to provide a context and a 'feel' for the way language is used; you can, of course, extract individual nouns or verbs from this to use in a different context. Entries considered to be more suitable for A2 level or equivalent are indicated in **bold** type.

- A list of related websites.

Unit 1 *Ich meine* lists words and short phrases for use in discussions (under 'Einfache Ausdrücke/Simple expressions'), then longer items for use in written work (under 'Längere Ausdrücke/Longer phrases').

Unit 19 *Welches Wort soll ich wählen?* lists key words for which English speakers often find it difficult to select the most appropriate German equivalent.

Learning vocabulary

Building one's active vocabulary quickly and efficiently (which also means remembering it!) is a major concern. Here is one technique for doing so. Always learn vocabulary at the beginning of a work session while you are still fresh.

1 Sit in a quiet place. No background music for this work!

2 Read each German–English pair of words or phrases aloud, twice, concentrating hard on the spelling as you do so.

3 After five pairs, cover up the English side of the page, and repeat the five pairs aloud again.

4 As stage 3, but this time cover the German side. Write the words out.

5 After 20 pairs, repeat stage 4. Repeat stages 3 and 4 after 2 hours, and again the next day. Give yourself a written test.

With practice, you will be able to learn 20–30 words in 10–15 minutes, and remember almost all of them weeks later.

Developing your vocabulary

Language is constantly changing. Jot down new words and expressions as you hear or read them; try to use the items in conversation or writing while they are still fresh.

Abbreviations in this book

Acc	Accusative
adj. noun	noun which works like an adjective
conj	conjunction
Dat	Dative
etw.	*etwas*
fem	feminine
Gen	Genitive
inf	informal, colloquial
insep	inseparable verb
invar	invariable case ending
irreg	irregular verb
itr	intransitive verb
jdn.	*jemanden*; shows that the verb or preposition takes the accusative
jdm.	*jemandem*; shows that the verb or preposition takes the dative
masc	masculine
nt	neuter
o.s.	oneself
pej	pejorative
pf	perfect tense
pl	plural
sing	singular
s.o.	someone
sth.	something
tr	transitive
*	perfect tense formed with *sein*

The vowel changes of less common strong verbs are given in brackets after the infinitive e.g. *treten (i-a-e)*

Feminine forms of professions etc. are, for simplicity's sake, only included where they vary from the usual addition of *-in* to the masculine form.

Paul Stocker

Allgemeine Seiten

www.statistik-bund.de   *Statistisches Bundesamt Deutschland –
statistical information on many aspects of German life*
www.destatis.de   *gleiche Seite wie oben*
www.inter-nationes.de   *Weiterleitung zur Seite des Goethe-Instituts*
www.tatsachen-ueber-deutschland.de   *Auswärtiges Amt – Tatsachen
über Deutschland*
www.linguanet.org.uk/   *Virtual language centre*
www.gfds.de/   *Gesellschaft für deutsche Sprache*
www.deutschland.de/   *das Deutschland-Portal*
www.bund.de   *Bundesverwaltungsamt*
www.forum-demographie.de/   *Forum Demographischer Wandel des
Bundespräsidenten*
http://www.statistik.at/   *Statistik Austria (Österreich)*

Contents

Introduction   iii

1 Ich meine ...   1

Einfache Ausdrücke   1

1.1   Erstens, zweitens   1

1.2   Dazu kommt noch ...   2

1.3   Zum Beispiel   2

1.4   Weil   2

1.5   Vor allem   2

1.6   Da habe ich Zweifel   3

1.7   Im Vergleich   4

1.8   Im Gegenteil   4

1.9   Meiner Meinung nach   5

1.10 Schließlich   5

1.11 Weitere nützliche Ausdrücke   6

Längere Ausdrücke   6

1.12 Einleitung   7

1.13 These   7

1.14 Antithese   8

1.15 Gründe geben   9

1.16 Schlussfolgerungen ziehen   9

Zeitausdrücke   10

1.17 Die Vergangenheit   10

1.18 Die Gegenwart   10

1.19 Die Zukunft   11

1.20 Verschiedenes   11

2 Menschliche Beziehungen 12

2.1	Die Liebe	12
2.2	Die Ehe	13
2.3	Trennung, Scheidung	13
2.4	Die Schwangerschaft	14
2.5	Die Familie	15
2.6	Alt werden	16
2.7	Charakter – Positives	17
2.8	Charakter – Negatives	18
2.9	Teenager über Eltern	18
2.10	Eltern über Teenager	19
2.11	Der Konflikt	21

3 Die Gesundheit 23

3.1	Gesund/ungesund	23
3.2	Körperliche Krankheiten	24
3.3	Die medizinische Behandlung	25
3.4	Der Sterbeprozess	26
3.5	Psychische Probleme	27
3.6	Das Rauchen	27
3.7	Der Alkoholkonsum	28
3.8	AIDS	28
3.9	Die Drogen	29

4 Der Tourismus 31

4.1	Unterwegs	31
4.2	Die Unterkunft	32
4.3	Auf Urlaub	32
4.4	Geographische Namen	33

5 Das Verkehrswesen 35

5.1	Die Verkehrspolitik	35
5.2	Die Straßen	36
5.3	Der Straßenverkehr	36
5.4	Das Autofahren	37
5.5	Verkehrsverstöße, Unfälle	38
5.6	Die Mitfahrer	39
5.7	Die öffentlichen Verkehrsmittel	39
5.8	Der Schienenverkehr	39
5.9	Der Flugverkehr	40
5.10	Die Schifffahrt	40

6 Sport und Freizeit — 42

6.1	Sportler	42
6.2	Sport und Wettbewerb	43
6.3	Der Sportgeist	44
6.4	Drogen im Sport	44
6.5	Die Freizeit	45

7 Die Medien — 47

7.1	Die Technik	48
7.2	Die Programmgestaltung	48
7.3	Probleme	49
7.4	Die Presse	50
7.5	Die Redaktion	51
7.6	Die Werbebranche	52
7.7	Die Werbepsychologie	53

8 Erziehung und Ausbildung — 55

8.1	Das Schulwesen	55
8.2	Lehrer und Schüler	56
8.3	Die Prüfungen	56
8.4	Der Lernprozess	57
8.5	Die positive Einstellung	57
8.6	Die negative Einstellung	58
8.7	Der Unterricht	58
8.8	Das Hochschulsystem	59
8.9	Die Sonderschule	60
8.10	Die Ausbildung	60
8.11	Die Bildungspolitik	61

9 Stadt- und Landleben — 63

	Die Stadt	63
9.1	Die Stadt	63
9.2	Die Städteplanung	64
9.3	Wohnungen	64
9.4	Probleme des Stadtlebens	65
	Das Land	66
9.5	Auf dem Land leben	67
9.6	Die Landwirtschaft	67
9.7	Die Zukunft der Landwirtschaft	68

10 Die Arbeitswelt   69

10.1 Eine Stelle suchen   69
10.2 Die Bewerbung   70
10.3 Das Vorstellungsgespräch   71
10.4 Die Geschäftsorganisation   72
10.5 Der Arbeitnehmer   73
10.6 Die Arbeitsbedingungen   73
10.7 Die Arbeitslosigkeit   74
10.8 Neue Arbeitsplätze   75
10.9 Frauen im Beruf   76
10.10 Die Gewerkschaften   76

11 Wirtschaft und Geschäft   78

11.1 Grundbegriffe   78
11.2 Die Wirtschaftspolitik   79
11.3 Das Steuerwesen   80
11.4 Die Firma   80
11.5 Der Geschäftsalltag   81
11.6 Angebot und Nachfrage   82
11.7 Aufschwung und Krise   83
11.8 Die Börse   83
11.9 Der internationale Handel   84
11.10 Mein Einkommen   85
11.11 Der Familienhaushalt   85
11.12 Die Banken   86

12 Die Politik   88

12.1 Die Staatsordnung   88
12.2 Die politischen Parteien   89
12.3 Der Wahlkampf   89
12.4 Die Wahlen   90
12.5 Das Parlament   90
12.6 Das politische Leben   91
12.7 Die Kommunalverwaltung   92
12.8 Die Europäische Union   92
12.9 Die deutsche Wiedervereinigung   93

13 Internationale Beziehungen   95

13.1   Die Außenpolitik   95
13.2   Der Krieg   96
13.3   Die Streitkräfte   97
13.4   Der Terrorismus   98
13.5   Die Dritte Welt   99

14 Soziale Fragen   101

Die Einwanderung   101
14.1   Flüchtlinge und Asylanten   101
14.2   Die Probleme für das Gastland   102
14.3   Die Probleme der Einwanderer   102
14.4   Der Rassismus   103
Die Religion   104
14.5   Glaube im Alltag   104
Die soziale Ausgrenzung   105
14.6   Die Armut   106

15 Die Rechtsordnung   108

15.1   Die Rechtsordnung   108
15.2   Das Privatrecht   109
15.3   Das öffentliche Recht   109
15.4   Die Gewalt   110
15.5   Die öffentliche Ordnung   111
15.6   Die Polizei   111
15.7   Vor Gericht   112

16 Die Umwelt   115

16.1   Die Probleme   115
16.2   Die Folgen   116
16.3   Die Gegenmaßnahmen   117
16.4   Die Luft   118
16.5   Das Wasser   119
16.6   Der Boden   119
16.7   Der Müll   120
16.8   Fossile Brennstoffe   121
16.9   Die Atomenergie   121
16.10   Erneuerbare Energiequellen   122
16.11   Konservierung zu Hause   122

17 Technik und Forschung 124

17.1 Die Hardware 124
17.2 Die Software 125
17.3 Das Internet 126
17.4 Die Kommunikation 127
17.5 Die Industrie 127
17.6 Die Forschung 128
17.7 Die Weltraumforschung 129
17.8 Die medizinische Forschung 129
17.9 Die Gentechnologie 130
17.10 Ethische Fragen 131

18 Das Kulturleben 133

18.1 Die Musik 133
18.2 Die Kunst 134
18.3 Der Film 135
18.4 Das Theater 136
18.5 Die Literatur 137
18.6 Kultur besprechen 139
18.7 Positives 140
18.8 Negatives 141
18.9 Neutrales 142

19 Welches Wort soll ich wählen? 144

1 Ich meine ...

20 Grundausdrücke	20 basic expressions
außerdem	apart from that, moreover
das mag sein, aber ...	that may be true, but ...
das stimmt (nicht)	that's (not) true
deswegen	that's why
eigentlich	actually
einerseits/andererseits	on the one/the other hand
erstens	firstly
es geht um ...	it's a question of ...
ich bin dafür/dagegen, dass ...	I'm in favour of/against ...
ich meine, ...	I think that ...
im Großen und Ganzen	on the whole
im Vergleich zu ...	in comparison to ...
jeder weiß, dass ...	everyone knows that ...
meiner Meinung nach	in my opinion
natürlich	of course
normalerweise	normally
sicher	certainly
was hältst du von ...?	what do you think of ...?
wie kommst du darauf?	what makes you think that?
zum Beispiel (z. B.)	for example

1.1 Erstens, zweitens   Firstly, secondly

am Anfang/zu Anfang	initially
erstens, zunächst	first/ly
schließlich	finally
das Pro und Kontra	the pros and cons
später	later
von vorn	from scratch, from the beginning
zum Abschluss	in conclusion
zweitens	secondly

1.2 Dazu kommt noch ...   And, what is more ...

auch	also
dazu	in addition
und dazu kommt noch, dass ...	and, what is more, ...
nicht nur ..., sondern auch ...	not only ..., but also ...
übrigens	incidentally, by the way
was ich eigentlich sagen wollte, ist ...	what I actually mean is ...
weiter	in addition

1.3 Zum Beispiel   For example

beispielsweise	for example (e.g.)
bekanntlich	it is known that
das heißt (d. h.)	that is (i.e.)
es stimmt, dass ...	it is true that ...
folgendermaßen	as follows
in Bezug auf (+Acc)	with reference to
in diesem Zusammenhang	in this context
jeder weiß, dass ...	everyone knows that ...
nämlich	viz., namely
die Tatsachen (pl)	the facts
unter anderem (u. a.)	among other things
wie	such as

1.4 Weil   Because

also, daher	therefore, so
da (conj)	since, as
dadurch, deshalb, deswegen	in that way, because of that, that is why
das liegt daran, dass ...	that's because ...
das hatte zur Folge, dass ...	the result of this was ...
ohne Folgen bleiben	to have no consequences
folglich	consequently, as a result
schon die Tatsache, dass ...	the very fact that ...
schon weil ...	if only because ...
solange (conj)	as/so long as
soweit ich weiß	as/so far as I know
Ursache und Wirkung	cause and effect
wegen (+Gen)	because of (sth.)

1.5 Vor allem   Above all, notably

es steht fest, dass ...	what is sure is that ...
ausgerechnet, wenn/als ...	just when ...
ausgerechnet er	he of all people
ausnahmslos	without exception

durchaus	absolutely, definitely
äußerst	extremely
bei weitem (das Beste)	by far and away (the best)
bei weitem (nicht so gut wie)	nowhere near (as good as)
besonders; zumal	in particular; especially as
betonen	to emphasise
eben; halt	just, simply
ganz und gar	completely, utterly
genau das	especially this
hauptsächlich	notably, mainly
in jeder Hinsicht	in every respect
keineswegs	not at all, not in the least
noch (bedeutender)	(even) more (significantly)
umso mehr, als	all the more, considering/as
umso wichtiger	all the more important
unbestritten ist, dass …	it's not disputed that …
sogar	even (*intensifier*)
möglichst (bald)	as (soon) as possible
(das musst du) unbedingt (machen)	(you) really (must do that)
völlig, vollkommen	completely
das Wichtigste ist es … zu (+*infinitive*)	the key issue is to …

1.6 Da habe ich Zweifel — I'm not so sure

abgesehen davon, dass …	quite apart from the fact that …
allenfalls; bestenfalls	at best
allerdings	even so/mind you
angeblich	supposedly, allegedly
auf den ersten Blick	at first sight
bis zu einem gewissen Grad(e)	to some extent
da habe ich Zweifel	I have my doubts there
einigermaßen	to some extent
es kommt darauf an, was …	it depends on what …
es sei denn, …	unless
gewissermaßen	in a way
ich habe den Eindruck, dass …	my impression is that …
kaum	hardly
keinesfalls	under no circumstances
lediglich	merely, simply
praktisch; quasi	virtual(-ly)
relativ	relatively
selbst wenn	even if
teilweise	partly
vermutlich	presumably
Zweifel ausdrücken	to express doubts, reservations

1.7 Im Vergleich — In comparison

ähnlich (+*Dat*)	similar to, like
als je zuvor	than ever before
ebenso	likewise
genauso	just the same
genauso wichtig	just as important
noch wichtiger ist ...	even more important is ...
kannst du das näher erklären?	can you explain that more fully?
sowie	as well as
vergleichen (ei-i-i)	to compare
verglichen mit (+*Dat*)	(when) compared with

1.8 Im Gegenteil — On the contrary

aber/jedoch	however
als Alternative	alternatively
auf der einen/anderen Seite	on the one/other hand
außer (+*Dat*)	apart from
da haben Sie schon Recht, aber	you are right there, but ...
dabei	at the same time/into the bargain
dafür	in return
dagegen	on the other hand
das hat damit nichts zu tun	that has nothing to do with it
das ist aus der Luft gegriffen	that's nothing to do with the facts
das stimmt auf keinen Fall	that's absolutely untrue
doch	however/though (and to contradict a negative question or statement)
egal ob ...	it doesn't matter whether ...
es ist fraglich, ob ...	it's questionable whether ...
es ist unvorstellbar, dass ...	it's inconceivable that ...
es kann sein, dass ...	it may be true that ...
freilich	admittedly
immerhin	all the same
in der Tat	in fact
in Wirklichkeit	in reality, in actual fact
mag sein, aber ... (*inf*)	that may well be, but ...
na schön, aber ...	that's all very well, but ...
obwohl (*conj*)	although
praktisch/in der Praxis	in practice
problematisch dabei ist ...	the problem with it is ...
sonst	otherwise
stattdessen	instead
trotz (+*Gen* or *Dat*)	in spite of
trotzdem; dennoch	nevertheless, despite this
überhaupt	anyway
während (*conj*)	whereas

was … angeht,	as for …,
wer das glaubt, …	anyone who believes that …
zugegeben; zwar	admittedly

1.9 Meiner Meinung nach   In my opinion

daran gibt es keinen Zweifel	there can be no doubt about that
du musst doch einsehen, dass …	you must agree that …
es geht darum, ob …	it is a question of whether
es geht um (+Acc)	it is a question of sth.
es liegt auf der Hand, dass …	it is obvious that …
es steht fest, dass …	it is certain that …
es versteht sich von selbst, dass …	
größtenteils	in the main
im Allgemeinen	in general
im Grunde	basically
in der Regel	as a rule
klar	clearly
kurz gesagt	in brief
kurz und gut	in a nutshell
offensichtlich	evidently
ohne Zweifel	undeniably
selbstverständlich	of course
zweifellos	doubtless
was sagst du zum Problem von …?	what's your view on the problem of …?
welche Einstellung hast du zu …?	what's your attitude to …?
wie ist deine Meinung?	what's your opinion?

1.10 Schließlich   Finally

das sage ich auch!	I think so too!
ehrlich gesagt	to be honest with you
es ist alles andere als …	it is anything but …
es ist schade, dass …	it is a pity that …
es ist unbegreiflich, dass …	it is inconceivable that …
es scheint, als ob …	it would seem that …
genau!	exactly!
glücklicherweise	fortunately
ich bin davon überzeugt, dass …	I'm convinced that …
ich schlage vor, (dass …)	I suggest (that …)
leider	unfortunately
die beste Lösung	the best solution
zu einem Kompromiss kommen	to reach a compromise
ganz meine Meinung!	that's just what I think!
mir scheint es so, als ob …	it seems to me that …
offen gestanden	quite frankly
ohnehin	anyway
schlicht und einfach	plainly and simply

Schlüsse ziehen	to draw conclusions
zum Schluss	in conclusion
so ist es!	that's right!

1.11 Weitere nützliche Ausdrücke   Other useful phrases

an sich	actually, on the whole
dadurch	in that way, because of that
dafür	in return, in exchange
irgendjemand	someone or other
irgendwann	(at) some time or other
irgendwas	something (or other)
irgendwie	somehow (or other)
irgendwo(-hin)	(to) somewhere or other
meistens	mostly, more often than not
mindestens	at least
ohne weiteres	straight away, without a second thought
nach und nach	bit by bit
sozusagen	so to speak
stellenweise	in places, here and there
teilweise	partly, in part
unerhört	incredible, outrageous
ungewöhnlich	unusual(-ly)
vielleicht	perhaps
wahrscheinlich	probably
weitgehend	largely
was ... betrifft	as far as ... is concerned

Längere Ausdrücke   Longer phrases

ein umstrittenes Problem	a controversial issue
das geht uns alle an	it concerns us all
wir dürfen nicht vergessen, dass ...	we must not forget that ...
es steht außer Zweifel, dass ...	it is beyond doubt that ...
im Gegenteil	on the contrary
es fehlt oft an (+Dat) ...	there is often a lack of ...
wenn wir es genauer betrachten	if we look at it more closely
um ein einziges Beispiel zu nennen	to take a single example
aus diesem Grund	for that reason
wenn man alles in Betracht zieht	all things considered
ich bin davon überzeugt, dass ...	I am convinced that ...

1.12 Einleitung | Introduction

alle sind sich darüber einig, dass …	everyone is agreed that …
an dieser viel diskutierten Frage scheiden sich die Geister	opinions are divided on this vexed question
angenommen, dass …	assuming that …
darüber wird heftig diskutiert	it has provoked a lot of discussion
das Für und Wider ⎫ das Pro und Kontra ⎭	the pros and cons
die Auseinandersetzung über … (+Acc)	the argument about …
die Meinungen über … (+Acc) gehen weit auseinander	opinions about … differ widely
ein nicht zu unterschätzendes Problem	a problem which should not be underestimated
eine heftige öffentliche Diskussion auslösen	to arouse intense public debate
eine heikle Frage	a thorny question
wir begeben uns auf gefährliches Terrain	we're entering a minefield
es ist zum Thema geworden	it has become an issue
es wird oft von anderen Themen in den Hintergrund gedrängt	it is often pushed into the background by the other issues
gehen wir davon aus, dass …	let's assume that …
in vieler Hinsicht	in many respects
ist das zu rechtfertigen?	can this be justified?
Kritiker bemängeln, dass …	critics point out that …
man gewinnt häufig den Eindruck, dass …	one often gets the impression that
man könnte meinen, dass …	one might think that …
plädieren für (+Acc)	to speak up for …
wir müssen uns damit auseinander setzen, was …	we must tackle the problem of what …

1.13 These | Arguments for

auf viel Kritik stoßen* (ö-ie-o)	to encounter a great deal of criticism
auf Widerstand stoßen* (ö-ie-o)	to meet with resistance
dank (+Gen or Dat)	thanks to
darauf wollen wir später zurückkommen	we shall return to this later
das Auffallende ist, dass …	the striking thing is that …

das muss man als wichtiges Anliegen erkennen	this must be recognised as an important area of concern
das Problem hat beängstigende Ausmaße erreicht	the problem has reached worrying proportions
die Folgen werden leicht unterschätzt	it is easy to underestimate the consequences
die Lage ... wird schlechter	the situation ... is getting worse
... erregt weiterhin Besorgnis	... continues to cause concern
... wird durch ... erschwert	... is made worse by ...
die Sache auf die Spitze treiben	to bring matters to a head
es ist leicht zu ersehen, dass ...	it is easy to see that ...
es ist nicht zu leugnen, dass ...	one cannot deny that ...
es wird zunehmend erkannt, dass ...	it is increasingly recognised that ...
etwas stimmt nicht mit ... (+Dat)	there's something wrong with ...
vom politischen Standpunkt aus gesehen	from the political point of view
was Sorgen bereiten sollte, ist ...	what should cause concern is ...
wir legen zu viel Wert auf (+Acc) ...	we attach too much importance to ...

1.14 Antithese   Arguments against

allerdings sollte man ...	however, we should ...
dagegen lässt sich einwenden, dass ...	one objection to this is that ...
das ist nur selten der Fall	that is only rarely the case
das ist zum Scheitern verurteilt	it is condemned to failure
das sollte man mit einem gewissen Argwohn betrachten	one should view this with some mistrust
der Sündenbock	scapegoat
die Gründe sind noch nicht endgültig geklärt	the reasons have not been fully explained
die Sache hat einen Haken	there is a snag
dies will nicht heißen, dass ...	this does not mean that ...
dieser Auffassung kann ich nicht zustimmen	I cannot accept this view
einer (Dat) Sache im Weg stehen	to be a stumbling block
er geht von falschen Voraussetzungen aus	he is arguing from false assumptions
es erwies sich als falsch	it turned out to be wrong
es gibt keinen Anlass zu (+Dat) ...	there are no grounds for ...
es kann leicht vorkommen, dass ...	it can easily happen that ...
ganz abgesehen davon ...	quite apart from that ...
geschweige denn ...	not to mention ...
man könnte annehmen, dass ...	one might assume that ...
seine Argumente kann man nicht für bare Münze nehmen	you can't take his arguments at face value
wir können uns der Tatsache nicht verschließen, dass ...	we cannot ignore the fact that ...

1.15 Gründe geben   Giving reasons

aller Wahrscheinlichkeit nach	by the law of averages/in all probability
aus folgenden Gründen	for the following reasons
aus politischen Gründen	for political reasons
gelten (i-a-o) für	to be true of
das gilt auch für ...	the same is also true of ...
das kann man an einem Beispiel klar machen/belegen	an example will illustrate this
die Sache auf die Spitze treiben (ei-ie-ie)	to bring matters to a head
die Statistik macht deutlich, dass ...	the statistics show clearly that ...
die Zahl wird auf ... geschätzt	the number is estimated at ...
es ist erwiesen, dass ...	it is a proven fact that ...
es wird geschätzt, dass ...	it is estimated that ...
in dieser/mancher Hinsicht	in this/many respect(s)
laut (+Gen or Dat) Gesetz	according to the law
laut Bundeskanzler	according to the Federal Chancellor (=Prime Minister)
man muss darauf hinweisen, dass ...	one must point out that ...
man vergleiche ...	let us compare ...
nach Erkenntnissen (+Gen) ...	according to the findings of ...
nach fachmännischen Schätzungen	according to expert estimates
wie oben erwähnt	as mentioned above

1.16 Schlussfolgerungen ziehen   Drawing conclusions

alles in allem	all things considered
das Entscheidende dabei ist ...	the decisive factor in this is ...
das ist erst möglich, wenn ...	that is only possible if ...
das kleinere Übel	the lesser evil
die Aufgabe ist es/besteht darin ...	the task is, ...
die richtigen Prioritäten setzen	to get one's priorities right
die Stichhaltigkeit des Arguments	the validity of the argument
diese Einzelmaßnahmen müssen mit ... (+Dat) gekoppelt sein	these individual measures must be linked to ...
einfache Lösungen gibt es nicht	there are no easy solutions
es bleibt uns nichts anderes übrig, als ...	we have no alternative but to ...
es lässt sich daraus schließen, dass ...	we can conclude from that that ...
es verlangt eine Umstellung unserer Einstellungen	it demands a change in our attitudes

ich bin der Ansicht, dass ...	I think that ...
man kommt unweigerlich zu dem Schluss, dass ...	one is forced to the conclusion that ...
man sollte sich vor Augen halten, dass ...	we should not lose sight of the fact that ...
ein Ziel im Auge behalten	to keep an aim in mind
Tatsachen ins Auge sehen (ie-a-e)	to face the facts
um diesen Gefahren vorzubeugen	in order to avert these dangers
um dieses Ziel zu erreichen	to achieve this goal
zum Scheitern verurteilt	condemned to failure

Zeitausdrücke   Time

1.17 Die Vergangenheit   The past

2006/im Jahr 2006	in 2006
anno dazumal	in the old days
bis jetzt	until now
bis vor kurzem	until recently
damals	in those days
das ist schon seit jeher so	it's always been like that
erst gestern	not until/only yesterday
in den letzten paar Jahren	in the last few years
in den 70er Jahren	in the seventies
in der guten alten Zeit	in the good old days
in letzter Zeit	recently (up to now)
längst	for a long time (past)
neulich	recently (not very long ago)
seit ewigen Zeiten	for ages
von Anfang an	right from the start
vor mehreren Jahren	several years ago
zu der Zeit, als ...	at a time when ...

1.18 Die Gegenwart   The present

aktuell	up-to-date, current
gleichzeitig	at the same time
heutzutage	nowadays
im Anfangsstadium	in the early stages
im neuen Jahrtausend	in the new millennium
im 21. Jahrhundert	in the 21st century
in der Nacht zum 24. Juli	on the night of the 23rd July
inzwischen	in the meantime
mit der Zeit gehen	to move with the times
momentan	at present
vorläufig	for the time being
es ist höchste Zeit, dass ...	it's high time that ...

1.19 Die Zukunft   The future

auf unbestimmte Zeit	for an indefinite period of time
früher oder später	sooner or later
für alle Zeiten	for all time
im Voraus	in advance
in naher Zukunft	in the near future
mit der Zeit	in (the course of) time
möglichst bald	as soon as possible
über Nacht	overnight
Versäumtes nachholen	to make up for lost time
von jetzt an/in Zukunft	from now on/in future
vorzeitig	ahead of time

1.20 Verschiedenes   Miscellaneous phrases

alle 10 Minuten	every 10 minutes
jede halbe Stunde	every half an hour
jeden zweiten Tag	every other day
das ganze Jahr über	all year round
den ganzen Tag	all day
die Altersgruppe (-n)	age group
er ist in den Vierzigern	he's in his forties
in den mittleren Jahren	middle-aged
sie ist Anfang/Ende zwanzig	she's in her early/late twenties
fast die ganze Zeit	most of the time
gelegentlich	occasionally
immer wieder	again and again
mit den Jahren	as one gets older
nach und nach	bit by bit, gradually
tagaus, tagein	day in, day out
zu jeder Zeit	at any time
zum ersten Mal	for the first time

2 Menschliche Beziehungen

mit jdm. ausgehen*	to take s.o. out, go out with s.o.
das Baby (-s)	baby
der/die Bekannte (*adj. noun*)	friend/acquaintance
der Ehemann (¨er)	husband
die Ehefrau (-en)	wife
das Ehepaar (-e)	married couple
die Eltern (*pl*)	parents
der/die Erwachsene (*adj. noun*)	adult
erziehen (ie-o-o)	to bring up (children)
der Freund (-e)	(male) friend, boyfriend
die Freundin (-nen)	(female) friend, girlfriend
geschieden	divorced
die Geschwister (*pl*)	brothers and sisters
heiraten	to get married
jdn. kennen lernen	to meet, get to know s.o.
das Kind (-er)	child
ledig	single
die Persönlichkeit	character
mit jdm. schlafen	to make love, sleep with s.o.
schwanger	pregnant
der Traummann/die Traumfrau	ideal partner
verheiratet	married
sich verstehen	to get on well with each other
der/die Verwandte (*adj. noun*)	relative
zusammenleben	to live together

2.1 Die Liebe   Love

jdn. anquatschen/anmachen	to chat s.o. up
ein Mädchen/einen Jungen ansprechen (i-a-o)	to talk to a girl/boy
anziehend, reizend	attractive
jdn. aufreißen (ei-i-i)	to 'pull' s.o.
braun gebrannt	(sun-)tanned
mit jdm. flirten	to flirt with s.o.
mit jdm. gehen*	to go out with s.o.
der Geliebte (*adj. noun*)	lover
das Verhältnis (-se)	relationship
sich in jdn. verlieben	to fall in love with s.o.
in jdn. vernarrt sein	to be infatuated with s.o.

an seinen Partner hohe Ansprüche stellen	to demand high standards of one's partner
jdn. auf einer Party kennen lernen	to meet s.o. at a party
jdn. um den kleinen Finger wickeln	to wrap s.o. round one's little finger
mit jdm. Schluss machen	to finish with s.o.
Liebe auf den ersten Blick	love at first sight
sich bis über beide Ohren in jdn. verlieben	to fall head over heels in love
sich einen Korb holen	to get the push
jdm. einen Korb geben (i-a-e)	to finish with s.o.
sie hat Angst davor, sich festzulegen	she's frightened of commitment

2.2 Die Ehe — Marriage

die Braut	bride
der Bräutigam	groom
die Gemeinsamkeit	common ground
die Hochzeit (-en)	wedding
die Hochzeitsreise (-n)	honeymoon
der Lebensgefährte (-n)/die Lebensgefährtin (-nen)	partner/common-law husband/wife
die Liebe	love
die große Liebe	the love of one's life, the real thing
der Polterabend	pre-wedding party
sich verloben mit	to get engaged to
die Verlobung	engagement
das Vertrauen	trust
die Zärtlichkeit	tenderness
die kirchliche Trauung	church wedding
die standesamtliche Trauung	civil ceremony
das gegenseitige Verständnis	mutual understanding
man sollte über alles sprechen können	you should be able to talk about everything
eine glückliche Ehe führen	to have a happy marriage
sie haben vieles gemeinsam	they have a lot in common

2.3 Trennung, Scheidung — Separation, divorce

der/die Alleinerziehende (*adj. noun*)	single parent
jdn. betrügen	to cheat on s.o.
auf jdn. eifersüchtig sein	to feel jealous of s.o.
der alleinstehende Vater	single father
die alleinstehende Mutter	single mother
die Eheberatung	marriage guidance (counselling)
Ehebruch begehen (*irreg*)	to commit adultery
die Einelternfamilie (-n)	single parent family

fremdgehen	to have affairs
sich trennen, getrennt	to split up, separated
die Promiskuität	promiscuity
sich scheiden lassen	to get divorced
die Scheidung	divorce
der Scheidungsprozess	divorce proceedings
der Seitensprung (¨e)	affair outside marriage
das Sorgerecht	custody
die hohe Scheidungsrate	high divorce rate
die meisten Geschiedenen heiraten erneut	most divorced people remarry
ein außereheliches Kind	an illegitimate child
er will sich nicht gebunden fühlen	he doesn't want any ties
auf Grund der Unvereinbarkeit der Charaktere	on grounds of incompatibility
häufig den Partner wechseln	to be promiscuous
ihre Ehe ging in die Brüche	their marriage broke up
sie hat ein Kind aus erster Ehe	she has a child from her first marriage
sie leben getrennt	they live apart
sie passen nicht zusammen/ zueinander	they're incompatible
zur Waise werden	to be orphaned
dem Vater wurde das Sorgerecht für das Kind zugesprochen	the father was awarded custody of the child

2.4 Die Schwangerschaft   Pregnancy

die Abtreibung (-en) der Schwangerschaftsabbruch (¨e) }	abortion
die Antibabypille (-n)	contraceptive pill
ein Baby stillen	to breast-feed a baby
der Buggy (-s)	pushchair, buggy
empfangen (ä-i-a)	to conceive
die Empfängnisverhütung	contraception
die Familienplanung	family planning
der Fötus (pl Föten/Fötusse)	foetus
die Fristenregelung	law allowing abortion within first 3 months
gebären (ie-a-o)	to give birth to
geboren werden* (i-u-o)	to be born
die Geburt (-en)	birth
die Geburtenkontrolle	birth control
das Kondom (-e)	condom
der Elternurlaub der Mutterschaftsurlaub }	parental leave (on birth of child)
mütterlich	motherly, maternal

das Patenkind (-er)	godchild
die (Antibaby-)Pille	contraceptive pill
der Schwangerschaftstest	pregnancy test
eine (un-)erwünschte Schwangerschaft	a(n) (un)wanted pregnancy
die Waise (-n)	orphan

ein Kind erwarten	to be expecting a baby
sie bekommt ein Kind	she's having a baby
ein Baby abtreiben lassen (ä-ie-a)	to have an abortion
in gebärfähigem Alter	of child-bearing age
die künstliche Befruchtung	artificial insemination
Mutter werden* (i-u-o)	to have a baby
zur Welt kommen	to be born
aus gutem Elternhaus stammen	to come from a good home
jedes 6. Paar bleibt ungewollt kinderlos	one couple in 6 is unable to conceive
der Schutz des ungeborenen Lebens	the protection of the unborn child

2.5 Die Familie   The family

ein Kind adoptieren	to adopt a child
autoritär	authoritarian
ein Kind erziehen	to bring up a child
der/die Erziehungsberechtigte (*adj. noun*)	parent, legal guardian
die Großfamilie (-n)	extended family
ein Kind verwöhnen	to spoil a child
Kinder großziehen	to raise a family
im Kindesalter	at an early age
der Kinderfreibetrag	child allowance
die Kinderjahre (*pl*)	years of childhood
das Kindermädchen (-)	nanny
die Kindesmisshandlung	child abuse
kindgemäß	suitable for children
die Kleinfamilie (-n)	small (nuclear) family
die Konfirmation/Erstkommunion	confirmation/first communion
der Pate (-n)/die Patin (-nen)	godfather/-mother
die Pflegeeltern	foster parents
das Pflegekind (-er)	foster child
der Schwager (⁻)	brother-in-law
die Schwägerin (-nen)	sister-in-law
die Schwiegereltern (*pl*)	parents-in-law
die Stiefmutter/der Stiefvater	stepmother/-father
streng	strict
die Tagesmutter	childminder
taufen	to christen

sie ist ein gut erzogenes Kind	she's a well-brought-up child
die permissive Gesellschaft	permissive society
die Verantwortung für Entscheidungen teilen	to share responsibility for decisions
die Verwandtschaft	family (all relatives)
von Kind auf	from childhood
was für eine Beziehung hat er zu seinem Vater?	what sort of relationship does he have with his father?
die Zwillinge (pl)	twins
das gefühlsmäßige Anklammern der Mutter an die Kinder	the mother's inability to let the children go emotionally
das gehört zu den Kindheitserinnerungen	that's part of one's childhood memories
immer mehr Ehen bleiben kinderlos	more and more marriages remain childless
die Schaffung emotionaler Geborgenheit	the creation of a sense of emotional security
die leiblichen Eltern	natural parents
das liegt in der Familie	it runs in the family
man soll Kinder zur Höflichkeit erziehen	children should be taught good manners

2.6 Alt werden — Getting old

das Altenheim (-e)	old people's home
die Altersbeschwerden (pl)	infirmities of old age
die Beerdigung (-en)	funeral
das Grab (⁻er)	grave
die Lebenserwartung	life expectancy
leiden an (+Dat) (ei-i-i)	to suffer from
in (die) Rente gehen* (irreg)	to start drawing one's pension
die Rente	pension
der Rentner	pensioner
die Senioren (pl)	senior citizens
der Seniorenpass (⁻e)	pensioner's bus/rail pass
sterben* (i-a-o)	to die
der Tod (-e)	death
die Witwe/der Witwer	widow/widower

in den (Vor)ruhestand treten* (i-a-e)	to take (early) retirement
in hohem Alter fit bleiben* (ei-ie-ie)	to remain fit in old age
sich an den Ruhestand gewöhnen	to get used to being retired
Frauen werden älter als Männer	women live longer than men
um jdn. trauern	to be in mourning for s.o.
die Radieschen von unten ansehen (ie-a-e)	to be pushing up the daisies
bis dass der Tod uns scheidet	till death us part

2.7 Charakter – Positives   Character – positive points

der Altruismus	altruism
anpassungsfähig	adaptable
begeistert	enthusiastic
bescheiden/die Bescheidenheit	modest/y
der Ehrgeiz/ehrgeizig	ambition/ambitious
ehrlich/die Ehrlichkeit	honest/y
die Eigenschaft (-en)	characteristic
extravagant	flamboyant
extravertiert	extrovert
fleißig	hard-working
geduldig/die Geduld	patient/patience
gehorsam/der Gehorsam	obedient, obedience
großzügig/die Großzügigkeit	generous/generosity
gut angepasst	well-adjusted
hilfsbereit	helpful
idealistisch/der Idealismus	idealistic/idealism
kinderlieb	fond of children
kontaktfreudig	outgoing
lebhaft, temperamentvoll	lively, vivacious
lieb/liebevoll	kind
liebenswürdig/die Liebenswürdigkeit	kind/ness
offen/die Offenheit	open/ness
rücksichtsvoll	considerate
ruhig	calm
selbständig/die Selbständigkeit	independent/independence
selbstbewusst	confident
sensibel	sensitive
sparsam/die Sparsamkeit	thrifty/thriftiness
sympathisch	likeable
treu/die Treue	faithful/ness, loyal/ty
unternehmungslustig	enterprising, adventurous
verantwortungsbewusst	responsible
vernünftig/die Vernunft	sensible/common sense
verständnisvoll	understanding
zielstrebig	determined, focussed
zurückhaltend	reserved
zuverlässig/die Zuverlässigkeit	reliable/reliability
ein braves Kind	**a well-behaved child**
einen guten Eindruck machen	**to make a good impression**
er ist lebensfroh	**he enjoys life**
er hat Humor	**he's got a good sense of humour**
gute Manieren haben	**to be well-behaved**
jeder Mensch hat etwas ganz Besonderes	**everyone has something special about them**

2.8 Charakter – Negatives   Character – negative points

aggressiv	aggressive
angespannt	tense
anstrengend	demanding
arrogant/die Arroganz	arrogant, arrogance
unsozial	antisocial
besorgt	anxious
blöd	stupid, idiotic
boshaft	malicious
brummig, grantig, mürrisch	cantankerous, grumpy
denkfaul	mentally lazy
deprimiert/die Depression	depressed/depression
egoistisch, selbstsüchtig	selfish
egoistisch/der Egoismus	selfish/ness
faul	lazy
geizig	mean (miserly)
gemein	mean (unkind)
gestresst	stressed
die Hemmungen	inhibitions
im Stress sein* (irreg)	to be under stress
das Labermaul ⎫ die Klatschtante ⎭	chatterbox, tittle-tattler
klagen	to complain
lügen (ü-o-o)	to lie, tell lies
nervig	annoying
reizbar	irritable
schmuddelig	sloppy
schüchtern	shy
unbeherrscht	lacking self-control
unehrlich/die Unehrlichkeit	dishonest/y
ungehorsam/der Ungehorsam	disobedient/disobedience
unverschämt	outrageous, impudent
verantwortungslos	irresponsible
verklemmt	inhibited
verschlossen	withdrawn
vulgär	vulgar
wahnsinnig	mad, crazy
wankelmütig/die Wankelmütigkeit	fickle/ness
er nimmt sich selbst zu ernst	he takes himself too seriously

2.9 Teenager über Eltern   Teenagers on parents

anständig	respectable
aufgeschlossen	open-minded
halten für	to consider (s.o.) to be …

sie hält ihre Eltern für ...	she considers her parents to be ...
– altmodisch	– old-fashioned
– autoritär	– authoritarian
– engstirnig	– narrow-minded
– gerecht	– fair
– heuchlerisch	– hypocritical
– (in)tolerant	– (in)tolerant
– kleinlich	– petty
– naiv	– naïve
– peinlich	– embarrassing
– scheinheilig	– hypocritical
– streng	– strict
– verkalkt (*inf*), muffelig (*inf*)	– senile, fuddy-duddy, grumpy
– verständnislos	– unsympathetic
– voreingenommen (gegen)	– prejudiced (against)
– wohlmeinend	– well-meaning
kompromissbereit	ready to compromise
schimpfen	to get cross
strafen	to punish
sich vertragen mit (+*Dat*) (ä-u-a)	to get on well with
vorwurfsvoll	reproachful

er geht mir auf die Nerven	he gets on my nerves
ich kann mit ihnen über nichts reden	I can't talk to them about anything
ich komme nur schwer mit ... zurecht	I find it hard to cope with ...
kleinliche Vorschriften	petty rules
man muss Respekt vor Älteren haben	you must respect your elders
meine Eltern bestehen darauf, dass ...	my parents insist that ...
Respekt zeigen vor (+*Dat*)	to respect
sie hat geschimpft, weil ich ...	she told me off, because I ...
sie können sich in meine Lage versetzen	they can put themselves in my shoes
sie nörgeln immer an mir herum	they're always nagging me
sie verstehen sich gut	they get on well together
sie sind stolz auf mich	they're proud of me

2.10 Eltern über Teenager   Parents on teenagers

sich schlecht benehmen	to behave badly
jdn. beschimpfen	to swear at s.o.
die Clique	one's group of friends
die Emotionen, Empfindungen	feelings, emotions
fluchen	to use bad language, to swear
gebildet	well-bred, educated

der Knigge	handbook of manners
kultiviert, fein	sophisticated, refined
lächerlich	ludicrous, ridiculous
die Markenklamotten	designer clothes
niedergeschlagen sein	to feel low
unmoralisch	immoral
verlegen	embarrassed
meine Eltern halten mich für …	my parents think I'm …
– apathisch	– apathetic
– ausweichend	– evasive
– deprimiert	– depressed
– gleichgültig	– indifferent
– hartnäckig	– stubborn
– launisch	– moody
– planlos	– lacking in direction
– überempfindlich	– oversensitive
– ungezogen	– ill-mannered
– unhöflich	– impolite
– unsicher, verunsichert	– insecure, uncertain
– verantwortungslos	– irresponsible
du nimmst deine Arbeit auf die leichte Schulter	you're not taking your work seriously enough
du willst das eine haben und das andere nicht lassen	you want it both ways
er ist total verdreht	he's all mixed up
er kommt mit seinem Vater schlecht aus	he doesn't get on with his father
gute Manieren haben	to have good manners
in den frühen Morgenstunden nach Hause kommen	to come home in the small hours
in den Tag hinein leben	to live for the day
sich in seiner Haut nicht wohl fühlen	to feel ill at ease
sie ist im Flegelalter	she's at that awkward adolescent stage
sich über etw./jdn. lustig machen	to make fun of sth./s.o.
sie malt alles schwarzweiß	she sees everything black and white
auf Äußerlichkeiten fixiert	obsessed with appearances
sich sonderbar kleiden	to dress outlandishly
die Verantwortung tragen (ä-u-a)	to take responsibility
alles in Frage stellen	to question everything
auf die schiefe Bahn geraten (ä-ie-a)	to go off the rails
aus dem eigenen Schaden lernen	to learn the hard way
das ist einzig und allein meine Sache	that's a matter for me alone
die Autorität in Frage stellen	to challenge authority

2.11 Der Konflikt   Conflict

angespannt	tense
ärgern	to annoy
ausziehen* (ie-o-o)	to move out
beleidigen	to insult
enttäuscht	disappointed
meckern	to moan, grumble
minderjährig	under-age
nachtragend sein	to bear grudges
reagieren	to react
jdn. reizen	to provoke s.o.
streiten (ei-i-i)	to argue, squabble
die Streitigkeiten (pl)	arguments
taktlos	tactless
ungelöst	unresolved
sich wieder vertragen	to make it up
jdm. (etw.) verzeihen (ei-ie-ie)	to forgive s.o. (for sth.)
zugeben (i-a-e)	to concede

die Beherrschung verlieren	to lose one's temper
bei etw. (+Dat) ein Auge zudrücken	to turn a blind eye to sth.
wir besprechen Probleme gemeinsam	we talk problems over together
ich bin nicht von gestern!	I wasn't born yesterday!
auf jdn. böse werden*/sein*	to get/be angry with s.o.
über etw. böse werden*/sein*	to get/be angry at sth.
ich falle mit der Tür ins Haus	I'll come straight to the point
sie gehen in die Luft (inf)	they fly off the handle, lose their rag
sie geht mir auf die Nerven	she gets on my nerves
es gibt Krach wegen ...	there's trouble about ...
viel Lärm um nichts	a storm in a teacup
das lasse ich mir nicht mehr gefallen	I won't put up with it any more
lass uns offen reden	let's be open about this
sie lässt sich von ihren Eltern nichts sagen	she won't be told anything by her parents
wir reden in aller Ruhe darüber	we talk about it quietly
das mache ich nicht mit!	I just won't stand for it!
ich nehme kein Blatt vor den Mund	I won't mince my words
ein Problem in einem offenen Gespräch lösen	to deal with a problem openly
Rechte und Pflichten	rights and responsibilities
sie reden nicht mehr miteinander	they're not talking to one another
mir reißt die Geduld	my patience is wearing thin

21

es steht eine unsichtbare Wand zwischen mir und meinen Eltern	there's an invisible wall between me and my parents
sie haben sich gestritten	they've had a quarrel, an argument
wir stimmen nicht überein	we don't agree
seinen Willen durchsetzen	to get one's own way
viel Wind um etw. machen	to make a fuss about sth.
ein wunder Punkt	a sore point
wütend reagieren	to react angrily
ich ziehe die Grenze bei (+*Dat*) …	I draw the line at …

Ehe

http://www.katholisch.de/3791.htm   *Katholische Kirche – die Ehe*
http://www.weddix.de/   *alles zum Thema Hochzeit und heiraten*

Trennung, Scheidung, Tod

http://www.postmortal.de   *der Tod in Deutschland in Realität und Rechtsordnung*
http://www.scheidungsfamilie.de/   *Ehe, Familie und Scheidung*

Schwangerschaft

www.profamilia.de/topic/F_uer_Jugendliche   *Deutsche Gesellschaft für Familienplanung, Sexualpädagogik und Sexualberatung e.V.*
http://www.svss-uspda.ch/   *Informationen zu Abtreibung*
http://www.abtreibung.de/   *Hilfe für ungewollt Schwangere*
http://www.bba.de/gentech/eschg.htm   *Embryonenschutzgesetz*

Familie

www.bmfsfj.de/   *Bundesministerium für Familie, Senioren, Frauen und Jugend*
www.familienhandbuch.de   *ein Internet-basiertes Handbuch zu Themen der Kindererziehung, Partnerschaft und Familienbildung für Eltern, Erzieher, Lehrer und Wissenschaftler*
http://www.prognos.com/familienatlas/   *Familienatlas 2005*
http://www.alleinerziehend.at   *Verein Allein mit dem Kind*
http://www.adoption.de/   *Informationsportal rund um Adoption*

Verschiedenes

http://www.kinder-ministerium.de/   *Bundesministerium für Kinder*
www.kindex.de/pro/index.aspx   *Kinder- und Jugendthemen*
www.jugendliche.de   *Webseiten für Jugendliche*
www.jugendhilfe.net/   *Diakonische Jugendhilfe*

3 Die Gesundheit

der Arzt (⁐e)/die Ärztin (-nen)	doctor
aufgeben (i-a-e) (tr/itr)	to give up
ausschlafen (ä-ie-a)	to lie in
Bewegung brauchen	to need exercise
sich erholen/die Erholung	to recover/recreation
sich fit halten (ä-ie-a)	to keep fit
gesund essen (i-a-e)	to eat healthily
krank werden*, erkranken*	to fall ill
der/die Kranke (adj. noun)	sick person
er musste ins Krankenhaus	he had to go to hospital
die Krankheit (-en)	illness
die Lebensqualität	quality of life
operiert werden* (irreg)	to have an operation
der Patient (-en)	patient
das Pflaster (-)	plaster, bandaid
Sport treiben (ei-ie-ie)	to do sport
die Tablette (-n)	tablet
trainieren	to train
bei einem Unfall verletzt	injured in an accident
verschreiben (ei-ie-ie)	to prescribe
verunglücken*	to have an accident
wohlauf sein	to be fit and well

3.1 Gesund/ungesund   Healthy/unhealthy

abnehmen/zunehmen (i-a-o)	to lose/put on weight
Ballaststoffe (pl)	fibre (in the diet)
die Essgewohnheiten (pl)	eating habits
fettleibig, die Fettleibigkeit	obese, obesity
der Fitness-Klub	health club
die Frauenklinik (-en)	well-woman clinic
die Frischkost	fresh food
das gesunde Essen	healthy diet
sich wohl/nicht wohl fühlen	to feel well/ill
das Gesundheitswesen	Health Service
das Junkfood/ungesunde Essen	junk food
kerngesund sein	to be as fit as a fiddle
die Körperpflege	personal hygiene

die Krankenkasse	health insurance company
die Krankenversicherung	health insurance
eine Kur machen	to go on a health cure
der Kurort (-e)	health resort
lebensnotwendig	essential
die präventive/kurative Medizin	preventative/curative medicine
die Menstruationsbeschwerden (*pl*)	period pains
die Periode (-n)	period
eine Schlankheitskur machen	to go on a diet
sie hat 10 Kilo Übergewicht	she's 10kg overweight
er bekommt nicht genug Bewegung	he doesn't get enough exercise
zu viel Fett und Zucker vermeiden	to avoid too much fat and sugar
vorbeugen ist besser als heilen	prevention is better than cure

3.2 Körperliche Krankheiten — Physical illnesses

sie hat eine Allergie gegen (+*Acc*)	she's allergic to
ansteckend	infectious, contagious
behandeln	to treat
der (Körper-)Behinderte (*adj. noun*)	(physically) disabled person
blind	blind
der Diabetes/die Zuckerkrankheit	diabetes
entdecken	to bring to light, detect
die Epidemie (-n), die Seuche (-n)	epidemic
sich erkälten	to catch cold
die Geschlechtskrankheit (-en)	sexually transmitted disease
die Grippe	influenza
heilen	to cure
nicht ganz auf der Höhe	a bit under the weather
sich ... holen	to catch ...
die Infektion (-en)	infection
der Keim (-e)	germ
leiden (ei-i-i) an (+*Dat*)	to suffer from
ohnmächtig werden	to faint
schmerzhaft	painful
stumm	dumb
taub	deaf
die Tropenkrankheit (-en)	tropical disease
das Virus (*pl* Viren)/der Erreger (-)	virus
die Wunde (-n)	wound
eine Untersuchung machen lassen	to go for a medical examination

3.3 Die medizinische Behandlung

Medical treatment

einen Arzt holen	to call a doctor
die Arzneimittel (*pl*) ⎱	
die Medikamente (*pl*) ⎰	medication, drugs
der praktische Arzt (⁼e)/	general practitioner
die praktische Ärztin (-nen)	
jdn. beatmen	to give s.o. artificial respiration
die Blutübertragung (-en)	blood transfusion
der Chirurg (-en)	surgeon
die Dosis	dose
der Facharzt (⁼e)/	medical specialist
die Fachärztin (-nen)	
geimpft werden*	to have a vaccination
die Hebamme (-n)	midwife
die Intensivstation	intensive care unit
der Krankenwagen (-)	ambulance
der Krankenpfleger (-)	(male) nurse
die Krankenschwester (-n)	(female) nurse
narkotisieren	to anaesthetise
die Nebenwirkungen (*pl*)	side-effects
der Operationssaal (-säle)	operating theatre
das Rezept (-e)	prescription
der Rollstuhl (⁼e)	wheelchair
röntgen	to X-ray
Schmerzen (*pl*) lindern	to relieve pain
das Schmerzmittel (-)	pain-killer, analgesic
die Schutzimpfung (-en)	vaccination
eine Spritze bekommen	to have an injection
die Tablette (-n)	pill, tablet
die Verpflanzung	transplant
die Vollnarkose	general anaesthetic
ein Medikament verschrieben bekommen	to be prescribed a drug
die örtliche Betäubung	local anaesthetic
jdm. strenge Bettruhe verordnen	to confine s.o. to bed

25

3.4 Der Sterbeprozess   Dying

alt werden*	to age
der Altersschwachsinn	senile dementia
die Arthritis/Gelenkentzündung	arthritis
der Bluthochdruck	high blood pressure
bösartig, gutartig	malignant, benign
die Euthanasie	euthanasia
die Grauzone (-n)	grey area (of law, morality)
die Herzkrankheit	heart disease
herzkrank sein	to have a heart complaint
die Herz-Lungen-Maschine (-n)	life-support machine
der Krebs	cancer
krebserregend	carcinogenic
Kreislaufstörungen (*pl*)	circulation/heart disorders
die Lebenserwartung	life expectancy
die Lungenentzündung	pneumonia
das Pflegeheim (-e)	hospice (for terminally ill)
rüstig	spritely
im Sterben liegen (ie-a-e)	to be dying
die Sterbebegleitung	terminal care
die Sterbehilfe	euthanasia
die Strahlentherapie	radiotherapy
die Todesrate unter (+*Dat*) ...	the death rate among ...
unheilbar krank	terminally ill, incurable
die Angst vor dem Sterben	fear of dying
an einem Herzinfarkt sterben*	to die of a heart attack
den Hirntod feststellen	to establish that s.o. is brain dead
nachlassende Kräfte	failing powers
dem Kranken ist nicht mehr zu helfen	the patient is beyond help
jdn. künstlich am Leben erhalten	to keep s.o. alive artificially
um das Leben kämpfen	to fight to keep s.o. alive
der menschenwürdige Lebensabschluss	a humane end to one's life
das Leiden unnötig verlängern	to prolong suffering unnecessarily
jdm. zum Selbstmord verhelfen	to help s.o. to commit suicide
im Vollbesitz seiner geistigen Kräfte	in full possession of one's mental faculties

3.5 Psychische Probleme   Psychological problems

die Angst (¨e)	fear, anxiety
ausweglos	hopeless
Beruhigungsmittel nehmen	to take tranquillisers
die Bulimie/bulimisch	bulimia/bulimic
die Depression (-en)	depression
deprimiert sein	to be depressed
die Essstörung (-en)	eating disorder
geisteskrank	mentally ill
die Magersucht/magersüchtig	anorexia/anorexic
die Nerven (pl)	nerves
der Nervenzusammenbruch	nervous breakdown
der Psychiater (-)	psychiatrist
psychisch gestört	emotionally disturbed
Selbstmord begehen (irreg)	to commit suicide
im Stress sein	to be stressed
die Telefonseelsorge	the Samaritans
verzweifelt sein	to feel desperate

mit den Nerven völlig am Ende sein	to be a nervous wreck
einen Nervenzusammenbruch erleiden (ei-i-i)	to have a nervous breakdown
an Schlaflosigkeit leiden (ei-i-i)	to suffer from insomnia
das Leben nicht verkraften können	to feel unable to face life

3.6 Das Rauchen   Smoking

asozial	antisocial
husten	to cough
inhalieren	to inhale
der Kettenraucher	chain-smoker
die Lunge (-n)	lung
an Lungenkrebs sterben	to die of lung cancer
der Nichtraucher (-)	non-smoker
das Nikotin	nicotine
nikotingelb	nicotine stained
paffen (inf)	to puff
das Passivrauchen	passive smoking
der Qualm	thick smoke, fog
der Raucherhusten	smoker's cough
er/sie stinkt nach Rauch	he/she smells of smoke
die Suchtkrankheit	addiction
der Teer	tar

außer Atem kommen* (o-a-o)	to get out of breath
sich (*Dat*) das Rauchen abgewöhnen	to give up smoking
seine Gesundheit schädigen	to damage one's health
seine Unsicherheit überspielen	to hide one's insecurity
eine Todesursache, die man vermeiden kann	an avoidable cause of death
das Rauchen verbieten (ie-o-o)	to ban smoking
die Werbung einschränken	to restrict advertising
vom Rauchen vergilbte Zähne	teeth stained yellow by smoking

3.7 Der Alkoholkonsum   Alcohol consumption

Alkoholiker sein	to be an alcoholic
die Aufklärung	education campaign
sich betrinken (i-a-u)	to get drunk
besoffen (*inf*), betrunken	drunk
der Blutalkoholspiegel	blood-alcohol level
seine Hemmungen verlieren (ie-o-o)	to lose one's inhibitions
der Kater	hangover
nüchtern	sober
das Rauschtrinken	bringe drinking
die Promillegrenze	the legal alcohol limit
das Rauschtrinken	binge drinking
die Sauftour/der Kneipenbummel	pub crawl
die Trunksucht	alcoholism
die Anhebung der Alkoholsteuer	raising the tax on alcohol
blau wie ein Veilchen	drunk as a lord
seinen Kummer mit Alkohol betäuben	to drown one's sorrows with alcohol
noch eins zum Abgewöhnen	one for the road
die Reflexe lassen nach	one's reflexes slow down
ins Röhrchen blasen (a-ie-a)	to be breathalysed
die Trunkenheit am Steuer	drink driving
einen Unfall verursachen	to cause an accident

3.8 AIDS   AIDS

das menschliche Abwehrsystem	the human immune system
an AIDS erkrankt	ill with AIDS
der/die Betroffene (*adj. noun*)	affected person
der Bluter (-)	haemophiliac
der Geschlechtsverkehr	sexual intercourse
HIV-positiv/-negativ	HIV-positive/-negative
der/die Homosexuelle (*adj. noun*)	homosexual, lesbian
die Immunschwäche	immune deficiency
der/die Infizierte (*adj. noun*)	infected person
sich verbreiten (*itr*)	to spread
zusammenbrechen* (i-a-o)	to break down

am schwersten betroffen sind ...	worst affected are ...
sich mit Aids infizieren	to catch Aids
durch Blut übertragen	to transmit by blood
die Zeit von der Ansteckung bis	the time from infection to the
zum Auftreten der Krankheit	appearance of the disease

3.9 Die Drogen   Drugs

aufgeben (i-a-e)	to give up
aussteigen* (ei-ie-ie)	to drop out
beschlagnahmen	to confiscate
der Cannabis, das „Gras", Haschisch	cannabis, 'pot'
der Dealer, Pusher	dealer, pusher
die Designerdroge (-n)	designer drug
die Droge (-n) ⎫ das Rauschgift (-e) ⎭	drugs (addictive)
der/die Drogenabhängige (*adj. noun*)	drug addict
der Drogenmissbrauch	drug abuse
die Ecstasypille (-n)	ecstasy tablet
das Einnehmen von Drogen	the consumption of drugs
die Entziehungskur	cure for addiction
die Entzugserscheinungen (*pl*)	withdrawal symptoms
Euphoriegefühle erzeugen	to produce feelings of euphoria
die Flucht	a means of escape
heroinsüchtig werden*	to become addicted to heroin
das Kokain, das Heroin	cocaine, heroin
legalisieren	to legalise
aus Neugierde	from curiosity
die Partydroge (-n)	recreational drug
im Rausch	under the influence of drink/drugs
der Rauschgifthandel	drugs trafficking
der/die Rauschgiftsüchtige (*adj. noun*)	drug addict
das Rehabilitationszentrum (*pl* -zentren)	rehabilitation centre
schnüffeln	to sniff (drugs)
sich (etw.) spritzen	to inject o.s. (with sth.)
stumpfsinnig	humdrum, monotonous
weiche/harte Drogen	soft/hard drugs
die Wirkung (-en)	effect
die Wiedereingliederung	rehabilitation
zittern	to shake, shiver

eine tödliche Dosis	a fatal dose
rückfällig werden	to go back (onto drugs)
vom Kokain runterkommen (*inf*)	to kick cocaine
auf harte Drogen umsteigen*	to move on to hard drugs
zur Abhängigkeit führen	to cause addiction

Der gesunde Mensch
www.bmg.bund.de/cln_041/DE/Home/homepage__node.html__nnn=true
   Bundesministerium für Gesundheit
www.bmgf.gv.at/   *Österreichisches Bundesministerium für Gesundheit*
http://www.bag.admin.ch/   *Bundesamt für Gesundheit (Schweiz)*
http://www.bfr.bund.de/   *Bundesinstitut für Risikobewertung*
http://www.dge.de/   *Deutsche Gesellschaft für Ernährung e.V.*
http://www.ble.de/   *Bundesanstalt für Landwirtschaft und Ernährung*
http://www.bzga.de/   *Bundeszentrale für gesundheitliche Aufklärung*
www.talkingfood.de   *Ernährung und Nahrungsmittel*

Körperliche Krankheiten
http://www.krebsinformation.de/   *Krebsinformationsdienst*
www.diabeticus.de   *Diabetes-Info-Server*
http://www.daab.de   *Deutscher Allergie- und Asthmabund e.V.*
http://www.drk.de/   *Deutsches Rotes Kreuz e.V. – DRK*

Die medizinische Behandlung
http://www.blutspende.de/   *DRK-Blutspendedienste*
http://www.stammzellspende.at/   *Stammzellspende in Österreich*
http://www.transplantation.de/ *Transplantationsmedizin*

Der Altersprozess
www.alzheimerinfo.de   *Informationen zu Alzheimer und Demenz*
http://www.igsl-hospiz.de/   *Sterbebegleitung und Lebensbeistand*

Psychische Probleme
http://www.depressionen.ch/   *Bewältigung von Depressionen*
http://www.psychotherapie.de/   *Psychotherapie, Psychoanalyse usw.*

Das Rauchen-/der Alkoholkonsum
http://www.rauchfrei.de/   *Nichtraucher werden – Nichtraucher Portal*
http://www.nichtraucher.de/   *Nichtraucher-Initiative*
http://www.anonyme-alkoholiker.de/   *Anonyme Alkoholiker*
http://www.alkoholratgeber.de/   *Das Alkohol-Gesundheitsportal*

AIDS
http://www.aidshilfe.de   *Deutsche AIDS-Hilfe e.V.*

Drogen
www.drogen-und-du.de/   *Schule, Jugend und Sport*
http://www.dhs.de/   *Deutsche Hauptstelle für Suchtfragen e.V.*
http://www.drogencom.de   *Drogen (für Jugendliche)*
www.drugcom.de   *gesundheitliche Aufklärung*
http://www.sucht.de/   *Fachverband Sucht e.V.*

4 Der Tourismus

das Abenteuer (-)	adventure
die Anmeldung (-en)	booking
der Aufenthalt	stay (e.g. in hotel)
sich ausruhen	to relax
besichtigen	to visit, look round (museum, etc.)
der Billigflug (ⁱe)	cheap flight
sich entspannen	to unwind
Europa bereisen	to travel round Europe
die Gaststätte (-n), das Restaurant (-s)	restaurant
mieten	to rent, hire
die Pauschalreise (-n)	package holiday
das Reisebüro (-s)	travel agent
die Sehenswürdigkeiten (pl)	the sights
der Strandurlaub	beach holiday
der Tourist (-en)/der Tourismus	tourist, sightseer/tourism
übernachten, wohnen	to stay (e.g. in hotel)
Urlaub machen	to go on holiday
der Urlauber (-)	holiday-maker
an der Küste	at the coast, by the sea
auf dem Land(e)	in the country
in den Bergen	in the mountains
ins Ausland fahren* (ä-u-a)	to go abroad
am Strand liegen (ie-a-e)	to lie on the beach
in die Ferien gehen* (irreg)	to go on holiday
ein Formular ausfüllen	to fill in a form
ich war 2 Wochen (lang) in Island	I went to Iceland for 2 weeks

4.1 Unterwegs — On the way

die Anreise (-n)	the journey there
der Ausweis (-e)	ID card
das Autobahnnetz (-e)	motorway network
der Charterflug (ⁱe)	charter flight
düsen* nach (inf)	to jet off to
das Ferienziel (-e)	holiday destination
der Langstreckenflug (ⁱe)	long-haul flight
reisekrank	travel-sick
der Reisepass (ⁱe)	passport
der Reiseverkehr	holiday traffic
storniert	cancelled

über ... fahren* (ä-u-a)	to travel via ...
verreisen*	to go away (on trip, holiday)
verspätet	delayed
übers/am Wochenende verreisen*	to go away for the weekend
mit wenig Gepäck reisen*	to travel light
auf eigene Faust reisen*	to travel under one's own steam
eine Weltreise machen	to go on a world tour
Zwischenstation machen in (+Dat)	to stop over in ...

4.2 Die Unterkunft   Accommodation

die Anzahlung (-en)	deposit (first payment)
sich aufhalten (ä-ie-a)	to stay
der Badeort (-e)	seaside resort
buchen/reservieren	to book, reserve
das Ferienhaus (-̈er)	holiday home
Gästezimmer (pl)	guest rooms (in guest house), vacancies
das Hotelgewerbe	hotel industry
die Jugendherberge (-n)	youth hostel
die Kaution	deposit (against damage)
der Kurort (-e)	health resort
das Luxushotel (-s)	luxury hotel
die Pension (-en)	guest-house
übernachten	to stay overnight
Vollpension, Halbpension	full board, half board
sich nach einer Übernachtungs- möglichkeit umsehen (ie-a-e)	to look round for somewhere to stay

4.3 Auf Urlaub   On holiday

abschalten	to switch off
sich gut amüsieren	to have lots of fun
der Ausflug (-̈e)	excursion, trip
ausspannen	to have a break
einpacken, auspacken	to pack, unpack
faulenzen	to laze around
der Fotoapparat (-e)	camera
ein Foto machen	to take a photo
fotografieren	to take photos
die Führung (-en)	guided tour
das Gepäck	luggage
in der Hochsaison	in high season
die Impfung (-en)	vaccination
sich impfen lassen	to have one's vaccinations
der Massentourismus	mass tourism
die Nebensaison	off-peak

der Pauschalurlauber (-)	s.o. on package holiday
der Reiseführer (-)	guidebook
der Reiseveranstalter (-)	tour organiser
der Rucksackurlaub	backpacking holiday
der Rucksacktourist (-en)	backpacker
Ski fahren gehen* (*irreg*)	to go skiing
der Skiort (-e)	ski resort
in der Sonne liegen (ie-a-e)	to sunbathe
der Strandurlaub	beach holiday
der Tapetenwechsel	change of scene
eine Tour machen	to go touring
die Tourismusindustrie	tourist industry
sich trimmen	to get fit
das Verkehrsamt, das Informationsbüro	tourist office
wandern gehen* (*irreg*)	to go walking, hiking

ich bin urlaubsreif	I need a holiday
wo fährst du in den Ferien/ im Urlaub hin?	where are you going on holiday?
die Auswirkung des Tourismus auf die Umwelt/die Einheimischen	the effect of tourism on the environment/local people
die Ferien auf dem Land(e) verbringen	to spend one's holidays in the country
Ferien vom Ich machen	to get away from it all
sich verwöhnen lassen	to allow oneself to be spoiled
ich verbrachte 2 Wochen in Russland	I spent 2 weeks in Russia
andere Länder erleben	to get to know other countries
den Horizont erweitern	to broaden one's horizons
ein Stützpunkt für Fuß- und Autowanderungen	a base for walks and car trips
die freie Natur	'the great outdoors'
die beliebtesten ausländischen Urlaubsziele	the favourite foreign holiday destinations
das Bedürfnis nach Erholung	the need for relaxation
sie verbringt ihre Wochenenden auf dem Land(e)	she weekends in the country
Terroranschläge haben einen erkennbaren Einfluss	terrorist attacks have an appreciable influence

4.4 Geographische Namen | Geographical names

die Ostsee	Baltic Sea
der Kanal/Ärmelkanal	the Channel
das Mittelmeer	Mediterranean Sea
der Pazifik	Pacific Ocean
der Bodensee	Lake Constance
die Donau	River Danube

der Rhein	River Rhine
die Themse	River Thames
Aachen	Aachen, Aix-la-Chapelle
Brügge	Bruges
Brüssel	Brussels
Dünkirchen	Dunkirk
Genf	Geneva
Genua	Genoa
Den Haag	The Hague
Köln	Cologne
Lüttich	Liège
Mailand/*adj.* Mailänder	Milan/Milanese
Moskau	Moscow
Mülhausen	Mulhouse
München	Munich
Neapel	Naples
Nizza	Nice
Nürnberg	Nuremberg
Straßburg	Strasbourg
Venedig	Venice
Warschau	Warsaw
Wien	Vienna
Bayern	Bavaria
Estland	Estonia
Island	Iceland
Lettland	Latvia
Litauen	Lithuania
der Schwarzwald	The Black Forest
Siebenbürgen (in Rumänien)	Transylvania
der Ferne Osten	the Far East
der Mittlere Osten	the Middle East (Iran to India)
der Nahe Osten	the Middle East

---

http://www.deutschland-tourismus.de/ *Deutschland-Tourismus*
http://www.deutschertourismusverband.de/ *Tourismus*
www.tui-umwelt.com *TUI Umweltmanagement*
http://www.fur.de/ *Forschungsgemeinschaft Urlaub und Reisen e.V.*
http://www.geografie.de/ *Literatur, Fakten, Daten*
http://www.dsw-online.de/ *Deutsche Stiftung Weltbevölkerung*
www.staedtetag.de *Deutscher Städtetag*
www.verreisen.de Ferienseite vom Hamburger Abendblatt
www.tte.ch Tourismus in Europa

5 Das Verkehrswesen

einsteigen*, aussteigen* (ei-ie-ie)	to get on, to get off
umsteigen* (ei-ie-ie)	to change (trains)
das Fahrzeug (-e)	vehicle
die Geldstrafe	fine
die Hauptverkehrszeit	rush hour
der Krankenwagen	ambulance
der Lkw (-s)	lorry, truck
die öffentlichen Verkehrsmittel (pl)	public transport
eine Panne haben	to break down
das Parkhaus (ⁱe)	multi-storey car park
der Pkw (-s)	car, automobile (official term)
der Stau (-s)	traffic jam
der Streifenwagen (-)	police patrol car
überqueren (insep)	to cross
einen Unfall haben	to have an accident
der Verkehr	traffic

5.1 Die Verkehrspolitik — Transport policy

die Beförderung	movement (of goods)
der Fernverkehr	long-distance traffic/heavy goods
die Geschwindigkeit	speed
die Grenze (-n)	border
der Kanaltunnel	Channel Tunnel
die Lkw-Maut	toll on lorries/trucks
die Neubaustrecke (-n)	new stretch (of road, track)
auf dem Parkplatz	in the car park
das Straßenbauprogramm	road-building programme
das Straßennetz	road system
die Sicherheit	safety
die Strecke (-n)	route, stretch of road
die Tiefgarage (-n)	underground car park
die Verkehrsberuhigung	'traffic-calming'
der Verkehrsinfarkt	gridlock
das Verkehrsministerium	Ministry of Transport
das Verkehrsschild (-er)	road sign
der Verkehrsverbund	integrated local transport system
das Verkehrswesen	transport and communications
vorhanden	present, existing
der Zeitgewinn	time-saving

das Netz ausbauen	to extend the network
für alle Fahrzeuge gesperrt	closed to all vehicles
den Pkw-Verkehr aus den Innenstädten fern halten	to ban cars from town centres
die Verkehrspolitik richtet sich nach dem Auto	transport policy is geared to the car
den Individualverkehr auf öffentliche Verkehrsmittel verlagern	to get private transport users to use public transport
sich an den Baukosten (pl) beteiligen	to share the building costs
die Kosten (pl) für etw. (+Acc) tragen	to bear the costs of sth.

5.2 Die Straßen   Roads

das Autobahnkreuz (-e)	motorway junction, intersection
die (Autobahn)auffahrt (-en)	slip road (onto motorway)
die (Autobahn)ausfahrt (-en)	slip road (leaving motorway)
der Engpass	bottleneck
die Gebühr (-en)	toll
die geschlossene Ortschaft	built-up area
der Knotenpunkt (-e) ⎱ die Kreuzung (-en) ⎰	crossroads, junction
die Einbahnstraße (-n)	one-way street
die Fernverkehrsstraße (-n)	trunk road
die Bundesstraße (-n)	'A' road
die Landstraße (-n)	'B' road
die Nebenstraße (-n)	side-road, minor road
die Ringstraße (-n)	ring-road
die Schnellstraße (-n)	express road
die Ortsumgehung (-en)	bypass
die Raststätte (-n)	service area
7 km kurvenreiche Strecke	bends for 7km
nach rechts abbiegen* (ie-o-o)	to turn off to the right
die Straße macht eine Kurve (-n)	there is a bend in the road
die Straße macht eine Rechtskurve	the road bends to the right
der Straßenbau	road-building
die Straßenbauarbeiten (pl)	roadworks
die Umleitung (-en)	diversion
einen Umweg machen	to make a detour

5.3 Der Straßenverkehr   Road traffic

die Autobahngebühr (-en)	motorway toll
mit dem Autoreisezug	by motorrail
der Berufsverkehr	rush hour/commuter traffic

das Einsatzfahrzeug (-e)	emergency vehicle
der Güterverkehr	freight traffic
die Hauptverkehrszeit	rush hour
der Individualverkehr	private transport
das Kraftfahrzeug (Kfz)	motor vehicle
der Last(kraft)wagen (-), Lkw	lorry, truck
der Lastzug (¨-e)/Fernlaster	juggernaut (US: truck-trailer)
der Lieferwagen (-)	van
die Lkw-Maut	road toll on goods vehicles
der Nahverkehr	local traffic
der ruhende Verkehr	stationary traffic
der Sattelschlepper	articulated lorry
der Schwerlaster (-)	juggernaut
der Schwerlastverkehr	heavy goods traffic
die Spitzenzeiten (*pl*)	peak periods
ein 20 km langer Stau	a 20km long jam/tailback
der Tankwagen (-)	tanker
den Verkehr lenken	to control/regulate traffic
eine hohe Verkehrsdichte	a high volume of traffic
die verkehrsreiche Straße	busy road
die Verkehrsstau (-e)	traffic jam
der Verkehrsteilnehmer (-)	road user
verstopft	congested
die Zunahme (an +*Dat*)	increase (in)
erhitzte/angespannte Gemüter (*nt pl*)	frayed tempers

5.4 Das Autofahren   Driving

der ADAC	≈AA/RAC
anschnallen	to fasten seat belts
die Anschnallpflicht/Gurtpflicht	compulsory wearing of seat belts
bremsen	to brake
den Führerschein bekommen (o-a-o)	to get one's driving licence
Gas geben (i-a-e)	to accelerate, put one's foot down
der geringe Benzinverbrauch	low petrol consumption
die Geschwindigkeitsbegren-zung (-en) das Tempolimit	speed limit
einen Helm tragen	to wear a helmet
der Kombi (-s)	estate car
die Limousine (-n)	saloon (US: sedan)
der Pkw (Personenkraftwagen)	car (official term)
rechts/links blinken	to indicate right/left
die Richtgeschwindigkeit	recommended speed limit (on motorways)
rückwärts fahren* (ä-u-a)	to reverse
der Sicherheitsgurt (-e)	seat belt

ein starkes Auto	powerful car
die Straßenverkehrsordnung	Highway Code
mit 100 Stundenkilometern (km/h)	at 100 km.p.h
überholen (insep)	to overtake
Überholverbot	no overtaking
unentbehrlich	essential, indispensable
verkehrssicher	safe, roadworthy
an jdm. vorbeifahren* (ä-u-a)	to pass s.o.
vorsichtig fahren* (ä-u-a)	to drive carefully
das Auto ist durch den TÜV gekommen	the car passed its MOT
der Führerschein auf Probe	driving licence for 2-year probationary period (for all new drivers)

5.5 Verkehrsverstöße, Unfälle   Motoring offences, accidents

abschleppen	to tow away
Abstand halten	to keep one's distance
das Blitzgerät (-e)	speed camera
auf etw. (+Acc) auffahren* (ä-u-a)	to drive into sth.
die Geldstrafe (-n)	fine
die Karambolage (-n)	multiple crash
die Radarfalle	speed trap
die Radkralle (-n)	wheel clamp
rasen*	to speed
der Strafzettel (-)	parking ticket (fine)
jdn. überfahren (insep) (ä-u-a)	to knock s.o. down
der Verkehrssünder	s.o. who has committed an offence
frontal zusammenstoßen (ö-ie-o)*	to collide head-on
der Zusammenstoß (⸚e)	crash, collision
der/die Verkehrstote (-n)	road casualty
ein Verkehrshindernis sein	to cause an obstruction
verunglücken	to have an accident
er wurde beim Rasen erwischt	he was caught speeding
ich wurde geblitzt	I was caught by a speed camera
das Limit überschreiten (ei-i-i)	to exceed the speed limit
auf der Stelle	on the spot
ins Schleudern geraten (ä-ie-a)*	to go into a skid
einen Unfall verursachen/haben	to cause/have an accident
er fährt zu dicht auf	he drives too close to the car in front
sein Führerschein wurde entzogen	his licence was confiscated
sie musste 100€ Strafe bezahlen	she was fined €100
die Unfallrate senken	to reduce the number of accidents

5.6 Die Mitfahrer

Passengers

jdn. absetzen	to drop s.o. off
sich auf den Weg machen	to set off, leave
die Fahrgemeinschaft (-en)	car pool, car-sharing arrangement
das Trampen	hitch-hiking
Mitfahrgelegenheiten	'lifts offered'
die Mitfahr(er)zentrale (-n)	agency for arranging lifts
jdn. mitnehmen (i-a-o)	to give s.o. a lift
ich bringe dich zum Bahnhof	I'll take you to the station

5.7 Die öffentlichen Verkehrsmittel

Public transport

alle 10 Minuten	every 10 minutes
einen Anschluss (¨e) verpassen	to miss a connection
der Busbahnhof (¨e)	bus station
die Busspur (-en)	bus lane
die Busverbindungen (*pl*)	bus services
fahren*, verkehren	to run (e.g. the bus runs)
halten (*tr/itr*) (ä-ie-a) ⎫ anhalten (*tr/itr*) (ä-ie-a) ⎬	to stop
jede halbe Stunde	every half hour
das Schienennetz	rail network
die S-Bahn, Stadtbahn	high-speed urban railway
im Stundentakt	at hourly intervals
der überfüllte Bus (-se)	crowded bus
eine verbesserte Linienführung	better service
der Verkehrsverbund	integrated local transport network
die Wochen-/Monatskarte (-n)	weekly/monthly travelcard

5.8 Der Schienenverkehr

Rail traffic

die Bahnverbindung (-en)	rail connection
belastet	heavily used
die Bundesbahn	Federal Railways
finanzielle Hilfen (*pl*)	financial help
die Subvention (-en)	subsidy
subventionieren	to subsidise
verstärkte Investitionen (*pl*)	increased investment
wenig frequentiert	little used
die Zeitkarte (-n)	season ticket
der Zuschlag	supplementary fare (e.g. 1st class)
zuschlagpflichtig	supplementary fare payable

dem Schienen- gegenüber dem Straßenverkehr Priorität einräumen	to give rail traffic priority over road traffic
das Schienennetz modernisieren	to modernise the rail network
eine Strecke stilllegen	to close down a line
das Defizit abbauen	to reduce the deficit
eine dichtere Zugfolge	more frequent train service

5.9 Der Flugverkehr · Air traffic

abstürzen*	to crash
der Billigflug (∵e)	low-cost flight
die Billigfluglinie (-n)	low-cost airline
die Bruchlandung (-en)	crash-landing
der Charterflug (∵e)	charter flight
einchecken	to check in
der Fluggast (∵e)	passenger
die Fluggesellschaft (-en)	airline
die Flugleitung/flugsicherung	air traffic control
der Flugschreiber (-)	flight recorder, black box
mit einer Höhe von …	at an altitude of …
er hat Jetlag (nt)	he's jet-lagged
landen*	to land
der Luftraum	airspace
der Pendelverkehr	shuttle service
die Startbahn/Landebahn (-en)	runway
starten*	to take off
der Zeitunterschied	time difference

5.10 Die Schifffahrt · Shipping

an Bord	on board
auslaufen (äu-ie-au)*	to set sail
die Binnenwasserstraßen (pl)	inland waterways
die Binnenschifffahrt	inland shipping
ertrinken (i-a-u)*	to be drowned
die Fähre (-n)	ferry
der Frachter (-)	freighter
die Gezeiten (pl)	tides
auf Grund laufen	to run aground
der Hafen (∵)	harbour, docks, marina
die Hafenstadt (∵e)	port
kentern*	to capsize
eine Kreuzfahrt machen	to go on a cruise
der Lastkahn (∵e)	barge
der Liniendampfer (-)	liner
die Massengüter (pl)	bulk goods
das Rettungsboot (-e)	lifeboat

Schiffbruch erleiden (ei-i-i)	to be (ship)wrecked
die Seeräuberei (-en)	piracy
die Seereise (-n)	voyage
die Überfahrt (-en)	crossing, passage
die Werft (-en)	shipyard
das Wrack (-s)	wreck
der Yachthafen (⏜)	marina

Die Verkehrspolitik
http://www.bmvbw.de/ *Verkehr, Bau und Stadtentwicklung*
http://www.bmvit.gv.at/ *Verkehr, Innovation und Technologie (Österreich)*
http://www.astra.admin.ch/ *Bundesamt für Straßen (Schweiz)*

Die Straßen
http://www.autobahn-online.de/ *Autobahnen in Deutschland*
http://www.toll-collect.de *Lkw-Mautsystem*
http://www.strassenverkehrsamt.de/ *Straßenverkehrsamt Deutschland*
http://www.dvr.de/ *Deutscher Verkehrssicherheitsrat e.V.*
http://www.verkehrsrecht-online.de/ *Informationen zum Verkehrsrecht*
http://www.dekra.de *Deutscher Kraftfahrzeug-Überwachungsverein*
http://www.vcd.org/ *Verkehrsclub Deutschland*

Das Autofahren
http://www.adac.de/ *ADAC*
http://www.kba.de/ *Kraftfahrt-Bundesamt*
http://www.vda.de/ *Verband der Automobilindustrie*

Die öffentlichen Verkehrsmittel
http://www.bahntechnik.de/ *Institut für Bahntechnik GmbH*
http://www.bahn.de/ *Die Bahn*
http://www.hochgeschwindigkeitszuege.com/ *die schnellsten Züge
der Welt*
http://www.lba.de/ *Luftfahrt-Bundesamt*
http://www.vdv.de/ *Verband Deutscher Verkehrsunternehmen*

Die Schifffahrt
http://www.binnenschiff.de/ *Bundesverband der Deutschen
Binnenschiffahrt e.V.*

6 Sport und Freizeit

der Ausflug (-̈e)	trip, excursion
sich ausruhen	to relax, unwind
der Druck	pressure
der Fan (-s)	fan
faulenzen	to laze around
gewinnen (i-a-o), siegen	to win
die Mannschaft (-en)	team
die Meisterschaft (-en)	championship
der Profi (-s)/professionell	professional/professional (adj)
das Spiel (-e)	match, game
spielen gegen (+Acc)	to play against
der Sport (pl Sportarten)	sport
Sport treiben (ei-ie-ie)	to do sport
die Sporteinrichtungen (pl)	sports facilities
der Sportler (-)	sportsperson
teilnehmen (i-a-o)	to take part in, to participate
der Tennisplatz, Fußballplatz etc.	tennis court, football pitch, etc.
trainieren	to train
die Turnhalle (-n)	sports hall, gymnasium
verlieren (ie-o-o)	to lose

6.1 Sportler   Sportsmen and women

der Athlet (-en)	athlete
der Fußballspieler, der Fußballer (-)	footballer, soccer player
der Gegner (-)	opponent
der Konkurrent (-en)	competitor, opponent
der Kapitän (-e)	captain
der Manager (-)	manager
das Mannschaftsmitglied (-er)	team member
der Profi-Fußballspieler (-)	professional footballer
der Schiedsrichter (-)	referee
Schiedsrichter sein*	to referee
der Sieger (-)	winner
der Spitzensportler (-)	top class sportsman
der Teilnehmer (-)	competitor
der Torwart (-e)	goalkeeper
der Trainer (-)	trainer, coach
der Verlierer (-)	loser

6.2 Sport und Wettbewerb   Sport and competition

ausscheiden* (ei-ie-ie)	to be knocked out (of competition)
die Bundesliga	national (football) league
das Endspiel um den Pokal/ das Pokalendspiel	cup final
entscheidend	winning (goal, point)
das Finale, Halbfinale (-)	final, semi-final
führen/vorn liegen	to be in the lead
die Fußballkrawalle (*pl*)	football hooliganism
der Fußballrowdy (-s)	football hooligan
die erste Halbzeit	the first half
kämpfen gegen	to compete against
das Mannschaftsspiel (-e)	team sport
Mitglied in einem Verein sein	to belong to a club
die Nationalmannschaft	national team
die Nationalelf	national (football) team
der Pokal (-e)	cup
das Rennen (-) ⎫ der Wettlauf (⁼e) ⎬	race
siegen	to win
der Spielstand	score
sportlich aktiv sein	to do sport
sportbegeistert, sportlich	keen on sport
der Sportplatz (⁼e)	sports ground
das Stadion (*pl* Stadien)	stadium
der Titel	title
der Vorlauf (⁼e)	heat
der Wettbewerb (-e) ⎫ der Wettkampf (⁼e) ⎬	competition
der Wettbewerbsgeist	competitive spirit
das Wettschwimmen, Wettsegeln etc.	swimming, sailing competition
das Ziel (-e)	finishing line
der Zuschauer (-)	spectator

ein Tor schießen (ie-o-o)	to score a goal
Satz und Spiel an X	game, set and match to X
um die Meisterschaft kämpfen	to compete for the title
den Pokal gewinnen	to win the cup
gegen jdn. laufen, schwimmen etc.	to race against someone
nicht in Form sein*	to be off form, off one's game
ein Foul pfeifen (ei-i-i)	to whistle for a foul
den zweiten Platz belegen	to come second
an erster Stelle	in first place
das Siegen wird zu wichtig	winning becomes too important
auf Sieg spielen	to play for a win
das Ergebnis war 3 zu 0	the result was 3–0
mit 3 Toren vorn liegen	to be 3 goals up

das Spiel endete unentschieden	the match ended in a draw
unentschieden spielen	to draw
wir waren ihnen haushoch überlegen	we completely outperformed them

6.3 Der Sportgeist — Sportsmanship

der Amateur (-e)	amateur
aufgeben (i-a-e)	to retire
disqualifizieren, ausschließen	to disqualify
das faire Verhalten, das Fairplay	fair play
die Herausforderung	challenge
der Leistungssport	competitive sport
manipulieren	to rig, fix
mogeln, schummeln	to cheat
die Olympischen Spiele ⎫ die Olympiade ⎭	Olympic Games
der Olympiamedaillengewinner (-)	Olympic medallist
der Sponsor (-en), sponsern	sponsor, to sponsor
das Sponsern	sponsorship
der Sportgeist/die Sportlichkeit	sportsmanship
der Teamgeist	team spirit
die Verletzung (-en)	injury
der Weltklassespieler (-)	world-class player
der Weltmeister (-)	world champion
der Weltrekordinhaber (-)	world record holder
der Weltumsegler (-)	round the world yachtsman

die internationale Verständigung fördern	to promote international understanding
den Rekord brechen (i-a-o)	to break the record
Sport ist ein Geschäft	sport is a business
die zunehmende Kommerzialisierung	growing commercialisation
sein Land vetreten (i-a-e)	to represent one's country
das intensive Training	intensive training
ein zweistündiges Training	a 2-hour training session
er geht jeden Tag zum Training	he goes for a work-out every day
ein Vermögen verdienen	to earn a fortune
er genießt Wettbewerbssituationen	he's a very competitive person

6.4 Drogen im Sport — Drugs in sport

sich aufputschen	to dope oneself
das Aufputschmittel (-) ⎫ das Stimulans (pl Stimulanzien) ⎭	stimulant
die Designerdroge (-n)	designer drug
die Drogeneinnahme	drug-taking

der Drogenmissbrauch	drug abuse
die Langzeitwirkungen (*pl*)	the long-term effects
die Leistungsdroge (-n)	performance-enhancing drug
leistungsfördernd	performance-enhancing
muskelaufbauend	muscle-building
die Nebenwirkung (-en)	side-effect
das Risiko (*pl* Risiken)	risk
sauber	clean (of drugs)

man fühlt sich unter einem enormen Druck	you feel you are under enormous pressure
die Drogen werden immer raffinierter	drugs are becoming more and more refined
eine Urinprobe testen	to test a urine sample
eine vom IOC verbotene Substanz	substance banned by the IOC
bei einem Sportler eine Droge nachweisen (ei-ie-ie)	to prove that a sportsman has taken a drug
ihm droht eine bis zu zweijährige Wettkampfsperre	he's threatened with a two-year ban
den Tests entweichen* (ei-i-i) den Kontrollen entgehen* (*irreg*) }	to be undetectable in tests
Athleten Kontrollen unterwerfen (i-a-o) (*insep*)	to subject athletes to tests
Doping kaschieren	to conceal doping
die Gesundheit riskieren	to endanger one's health
der Erfolg um jeden Preis	success at all costs

6.5 Die Freizeit — Free time

sich entspannen	to relax, unwind
basteln	to make things, do crafts
das Brettspiel (-e)	board game
sich fit machen/halten (ä-ie-a)	to get/keep fit
das Fitnesscenter	fitness centre
sich von allem frei machen	to get away from it all
im Freien	in the open air
ins Freie gelangen*	to get out into the fresh air
die Freizeitindustrie	leisure industry
die Freizeitgestaltung	organisation of one's leisure time
das Gesellschaftsspiel (-e)	party game
das Hobby die Freizeitbeschäftigung (-en) }	leisure activity, hobby
die körperliche Aktivität	physical activity
das Lotto	(National) lottery
der Verein (-e)	club, association
Veranstaltungen (*pl*)	'what's on?'; events
wetten	to bet
die Wochenendreise (-n)	weekend trip

Zeit für sich haben	to have time to oneself
ich bin Mitglied in ...	I'm a member of ...
im Lotto gewinnen (i-a-o)	to win the lottery
Berlin hat einen hohen Freizeitwert	Berlin has a lot to offer in the way of leisure activities
ein langes Wochenende machen	to take a long weekend
ein breites Freizeitangebot machen	to offer a wide range of leisure activities
spielen wir ein bisschen Tennis?	how about a quick game of tennis?
aus der Form geraten* (ä-ie-a)	to get out of condition
sein Gewicht reduzieren } **abnehmen (i-a-o)**	to reduce one's weight
sich mit anderen messen	to measure oneself against others
man braucht viel teure Ausrüstung	you need a lot of expensive kit

www.sport.de   *RTL Sport-Rubrik*
http://www.cricket.de   *Deutscher Cricket Bund*
http://www.deb-online.de/   *Deutscher Eishockey-Bund e.V.*
http://www.dhb.de/   *Deutscher Handballbund*
www.leichtathletik.de   *Deutscher Leichtathletik-Verband*
www.rad-net.de   *Bund Deutscher Radfahrer e.V.*
http://www.rugby.de   *Deutscher Rugby-Verband*
www.dtb-tennis.de   *Deutscher Tennis Bund*
http://www.dsb.de/   *Deutscher Sportbund*
http://www.dsv-bfg.de   *Breiten-, Freizeit- und Gesundheitssport*
http://www.sportgate.de/   *Informationen über allgemeine Sportarten*
http://www.ski-online.de/   *Deutscher Skiverband*
http://www.dsv.de/   *Deutscher Schwimm-Verband e.V.*
http://www.segel.de   *das Segeln-Portal*
http://www.nada-bonn.de/   *Nationale Anti-Doping-Agentur*
http://www.dopingnews.de/   *Dopingnews*
http://www.freizeitnetz.de/   *Freizeitnetz – das Freizeitportal*
http://www.freizeitpark.de/   *Parkscout – Freizeitspaß online*

7 Die Medien

der Actionfilm (-e)	action film
aktuell	up to date
der Artikel (-n)	article
der Bericht (-er)	report
das Bild (-er)	picture
die Dokumentarsendung (-en)	documentary
einschalten, ausschalten	to switch on, to switch off
fernsehen (ie-a-e)	to watch TV
das Fernsehen/im Fernsehen	television (the medium)/on TV
die Serie (-n)	series
die Soap (-s) die Seifenoper (-n) }	soap opera
die (Sende-)Folge	episode
informieren	to inform
der Journalist (-en)	journalist
ins Kino gehen* *(irreg)*	to go to the cinema
der Leser/lesen (ie-a-e)	reader/to read
das Massenmedium *(pl* -medien)	mass medium
die Nachricht	(item of) news
die Presse	the press
das Radio/im Radio	radio/on the radio
der Rundfunk	broadcasting
die Schlagzeile (-n)	headline
die Seite (-n)	page
die Sendereihe (-n)	series
die Sendung (-en)	broadcast, programme
der Spielfilm (-e)	feature film
die Spielshow (-s)	game show
die Sportschau (-en)	sports programme
die Tagesschau	the news
die Talkshow (-s)	chat show
das Videospiel (-e)	video game
der Werbespot (-s)	advertisement (on TV, radio)
die Werbung	advertising
der Zeichentrickfilm (-e)	cartoon film
die Zeitschrift (-en)	magazine
die Zeitung (-en)	newspaper

7.1 Die Technik | Technology

anschließen (ie-o-o)	to plug in
aufzeichnen, aufnehmen	to record
die Aufnahme (-n)	recording
der Bildschirm (-e)	screen
der CD-/DVD-/MP3-Spieler (-)	CD/DVD/MP3 player
das Digitalfernsehen	digital television
empfangen (ä-i-a)	to receive
der Fernsehapparat ⎱ der Fernseher ⎰	television (set)
die Fernbedienung	remote control
herausziehen (ie-o-o)	to unplug
das Satellitenfernsehen	satellite television
hochauflösendes Fernsehen	high-definition TV
der Hörfunk	radio
das Kabelfernsehen	cable television
über Kabel übertragen (ä-u-a) (insep)	to transmit by cable
der Kanal (¨e)	channel
die Lokalradiostation (-en)	local radio station
die Parabolantenne (-n)	satellite dish
der LCD-/Plasmabildschirm	LCD/plasma screen
senden/der Sender (-)	to broadcast/station
die Stereoanlage (-n)	hi-fi system
umschalten auf (+Acc)	to change channels to
der Videotext/Bildschirmtext	teletext
die Videokamera (-s)	video camera
der Videorekorder (-)	video recorder
zappen	to flick from one channel to another
das Heimkino	home cinema

7.2 Die Programmgestaltung | Programmes

der Ansager (-)	announcer
das Frühstücksfernsehen	breakfast television
das Interview (-s)	interview
interviewen (pf: hat … interviewt)	to interview
der Krimi (-s)	crime/detective film
Kultur…	cultural
Lehr…	educational
live	live
der Moderator	presenter
die aktuelle Sendung	current affairs programme
die Nachrichtensendung (-en) ⎱ die Tagesschau ⎰	news
der Nachrichtensprecher (-)	newsreader
das Programm (-e)	channel/programme guide

die Realityshow (-s)	reality show
das Schulfernsehen	broadcasting for schools
synchronisiert, mit Untertiteln	dubbed, with subtitles
die Talkshow (-s)	chat show
der Überblick	summary
unterhalten (ä-ie-a) *(insep)*	to entertain
die Unterhaltungssendung (-en)	entertainment programme
die Verkehrsmeldung (-en)	traffic report
die Wiederholung (-en)	repeat
zum x-ten Mal	for the *n*th time
die Vielfalt	great variety
die Zuschauerzahlen *(pl)* ⎱	viewing figures
die Einschaltquote (-n) ⎰	
der Werbeblock (⁼e)	commercial break
die Wettervorhersage	weather forecast
der Zuschauer (-)	viewer *(pl:* also audience)
der Zuhörer (-)	listener *(pl:* also audience)

„Sie hören Nachrichten"	'here is the news' (radio)
mit den Nachrichten auf dem Laufenden bleiben* (ei-ie-ie)	to keep up to date with the news
wie soeben gemeldet wird	according to reports just coming in
Live-Sendungen lassen den Zuschauer am aktuellen Geschehen teilhaben	live broadcasts allow the viewer to keep up with events as they happen
sich durch Werbeeinnahmen finanzieren	to be financed by advertising revenue
ein erweitertes Angebot von Sendungen vorführen	to show a greater range of programmes
was kommt heute Abend im Fernsehen?	what's on television this evening?

7.3 Probleme — Problems

eine Alternative bieten (ie-o-o)	to offer an alternative
die Auswirkung auf (+*Acc*)	the effect on
beeinflussen	to influence
die Brutalität	brutality
die Couchpotato (-s) ⎱	couch potato
der Dauerglotzer (-) ⎰	
gewaltsam	violent
die unkritische Haltung	uncritical attitude
die heile Familie	secure, normal family
passiv	passive
die Pornographie	pornography
die Scheinwelt	a bogus world
die Schießerei	shooting, shoot-out

kreative Tätigkeiten (*pl*)	creative activities
trivial	trivial
verbreiten	to disseminate
das Verhalten	behaviour
verharmlosen	to make sth. appear harmless
der Verlust von Phantasie/ Phantasieverlust	loss of one's imagination
wertlos	worthless
vertrotteln (*inf*), vegetieren	to vegetate

es lässt dich verdummen	it dulls your mind
sie klebt am Fernseher	she's glued to the set
sie verherrlichen die Gewalt	they glorify violence
es beeinflusst unsere Wertvorstellungen	it influences our moral values
besteht ein direkter Zusammenhang zwischen Gewaltdarstellungen und Jugendkriminalität?	is there a direct link between the depiction of violence and teenage crime?
eine über die Medien transportierte Tolerierung der Gewalt	a tolerance of violence conveyed by the media
es steht im Mittelpunkt pädagogischer Kritik	it is at the centre of criticism from educationalists
hier wird keine heile Welt vorgeführt	there's no utopia shown here
sie wenden viel zu viel Zeit für Fernsehen auf	they spend far too much time watching television
Eltern sollten verhindern, dass Kinder ...	parents should prevent their children from ...
sie beschäftigen sich zu wenig mit ihren Kindern	they take too little interest in their children

7.4 Die Presse   The press

abonnieren/der Abonnent (-en)	to subscribe to/subscriber
das Jahresabonnement	a year's subscription
das Anzeigenblatt (¨er)	local advertising paper
die Auflage	circulation
auflagenstark	with a big circulation
die Ausgabe (-n)	edition
die Boulevardpresse	gutter press
die Boulevardzeitung (-en)	tabloid paper
das Comic-Heft (-e)	comic
durchblättern (*insep*)	to flick through
erscheinen* (ei-ie-ie)	to be published
bei Hodder erschienen	published by Hodder
die Illustrierte (-n)	magazine

das Fachblatt (⸚er)	specialist magazine
das Käseblatt (⸚er) *(inf)*	local rag *(inf)*
die Leserschaft	readership
monatlich	monthly
die Ortszeitung (-en)	local paper
die Presseagentur (-en)	press agency
die Pressekonzentration	ownership of the press by a few
die Pressezensur/zensieren	censorship/to censor
die Regenbogenpresse	trashy magazines
der Verlag (-e)	publishing company
wöchentlich	weekly
eine Zeitung herausgeben (i-a-e)	to publish a newspaper
der Zeitungshändler (-)	newsagent
die überregionale Zeitung (-en)	national newspaper

7.5 Die Redaktion   Editing

aktuelle Ereignisse	current events
von aktuellem Interesse	of current interest
die Aufmachung	presentation, layout
der Augenzeuge (-n)	eye witness
ausführlich	full, detailed
die Balkenüberschrift (-en)	banner headline
berichten über (+*Acc*)⎫ melden ⎬	to report
der Bericht (-e), die Meldung (-en)	report
die Berichterstattung	reporting
die Enthüllungen *(pl)*	revelations
der Enthüllungsjournalismus	investigative journalism
das Ereignis (-se)/sich ereignen	event/to happen
geschehen* (ie-a-e) ⎫ vorgehen* *(irreg)*/sich abspielen ⎬	to take place, happen
das Feuilleton (-s)	feature/review/arts section
das Titelblatt (⸚er)	front page
informativ	informative
das Inserat (-e)	small ad
die Klatschspalte (-n)	gossip column
der Knüller	scoop
die Kolumne (-n)	column (article and page division)
der Kommentar	comment, analysis
etw. kommentieren	to comment on sth.
die Kritik (-en)	critique, critical review
der Kritiker (-)	critic
das Layout	layout
der Leserbrief (-e)	readers' letters
der Leitartikel (-)	leading article

die Lokalnachrichten (*pl*)	local news
die Meinungsumfrage (-n)	opinion poll
der Nachruf (-e)	obituary
die Pressefreiheit	freedom of the press
die Pressekonferenz (-en)	press conference
die Problemseite (-n) ⎱ der Kummerkasten (-̈) ⎰	problem page
der Redakteur (-e)	editor
die Redaktion	editorial staff
reißerisch	sensational
die Reportage	(longer, fuller) report
der Reporter (-)	reporter
die Rezension (-en)	review
richtunggebend	influential
sachlich, objektiv	objective
Schlagzeilen machen	to hit the headlines
die Sportseite (-n)	sports page
subjektiv, unsachlich	subjective
„Veranstaltungen"	'what's on?'
die Verleumdung	libel
vertuschen	to hush up
voreingenommen	biased
die Werbung, die Reklame	advertising

die Presse mundtot machen	to gag the press
eine Presseerklärung herausgeben (i-a-e)	to release a press statement
etw. einseitig schildern	to report sth. in a biased way
ein Zerrbild entwerfen (i-a-o)	to give a distorted picture
sich/einen auf dem Laufenden halten (ä-ie-a)	to keep o.s./s.o. up to date
seine Macht missbrauchen	to abuse one's power
sie greifen (ei-i-i) in die Privatsphäre ein	they invade people's privacy

**eine Zeitung auf Schadenersatz
  verklagen**
	to claim damages from
	  a newspaper

**es stellt eine Gefahr für die
  Meinungsvielfalt dar**
	it threatens to restrict the
	  expression of a variety of opinions

7.6 Die Werbebranche   The advertising industry

die Anschlagtafel (-n)	advertising hoarding
die Kleinanzeige (-n)	small ad
die Konsumgesellschaft	consumer society
der Konsument (*weak noun*) ⎱ der Verbraucher (-) ⎰	consumer
der Lebensstil	life-style
die Marktforschung	market research

den Markt sättigen	to saturate the market
die Plakatwand (¨e)	hoarding/billboard
der Medienrummel	media hype
werben (i-a-o) für	to promote
die Werbeagentur (-en)	advertising agency
die Werbeaktion (-en)	advertising campaign
die Werbeausgaben (pl)	expenditure on advertising
die Werbeaussage	advertising message
das Werbefernsehen	television advertising
der Werbegag (-s)	stunt
die Werbekampagne (-n)	advertising campaign
der Werbeslogan (-s)	advertising slogan
der Werbeträger (-)	advertising medium
werbewirksam sein*	to have good publicity value
zielen auf (+Acc)	to target
die Zielgruppe (-n)	target group
die Aufmerksamkeit auf ein Produkt lenken	to draw attention to a product
der Markt ist hart umkämpft	there is strong competition
ein Produkt auf den Markt bringen	to bring out a product
sie erfüllen alle dieselbe Funktion	they all do the same thing
über seine Verhältnisse leben	to live beyond one's means
die Kaufkraft der Jugendlichen	the purchasing power of young people

7.7 Die Werbepsychologie   Advertising psychology

etw. ansprechen (i-a-o)	to appeal to sth.
ausnutzen	to take advantage of
ausbeuten	to exploit, use
als Blickfang	to catch the eye
Erwartungen prägen	to shape expectations
etw. groß herausbringen (irreg)	to hype something up
sein Image verbessern	to improve one's image
die niederen Instinkte	our baser instincts
zum Kauf animieren	to motivate people to buy
die Kauflust	desire to buy things
der Konsumterror	pressures of consumer society
der Konsumzwang	pressure to buy unnecessary goods
das Markenbild (-er)	image (of product)
die Markenwiedererkennung	brand recognition
überreden	to persuade
überzeugen	to convince
überzeugend	persuasive
unbewusst	subconscious
verführen	to tempt

einen positiven Eindruck erwecken	to give a favourable impression
Ansprüche, die nicht zu erfüllen sind	demands which cannot be met
Konsumbedürfnisse wecken	to create needs
sich ein Statussymbol anschaffen	to acquire/purchase a status symbol
Waren mit erstrebenswerten Eigenschaften verknüpfen	to link a product to desirable qualities
Prominente werden eingesetzt, um einem Produkt Prestige zu verleihen (ei-ie-ie)	well-known people are used to give a product some prestige

---

Der Rundfunk
http://www.dra.de/   *Stiftung Deutsches Rundfunkarchiv*
http://www.digitv.de/   *Digitalfernsehen*
www.agf.de   *Arbeitsgemeinschaft Fernsehforschung*

Die Presse
http://www.faz.net   *Frankfurter Allgemeine Zeitung*
http://www.welt.de/   *Die Welt*
http://www.virtourist.com/newspapers/europe.htm   *Linkliste Newspapers*
www.bild.de   *BILD-Zeitung*
www.derstandard.at   *Der Standard*
www.reporter-ohne-grenzen.de   *Reporter ohne Grenzen e.V.*
http://www.dpa.de   *Deutsche Presse-Agentur*
www.focus.de   *Nachrichtenmagazin*

Die Werbung
http://www.werbung.at/   *Informationen über die Werbung*
www.zaw.de   *Zentralverband der deutschen Werbewirtschaft*

Verschiedenes
http://www.medien-links.de/   *Deutschsprachige Medien-Links*

8 Erziehung und Ausbildung

das Abitur (*no pl*)	'A' levels, Higher Grades
aufschreiben (ei-ie-ie)	to note (down)
sein Bestes tun (u-a-a)	to do one's best
ich bin gut in Englisch	I'm good at English
der Erfolg	success
erklären	to explain
die Erziehung	education, upbringing
die Ganztagsschule (-n)	all-day school/schooling
die Gesamtschule (-n)	comprehensive school
das Gymnasium (*pl* Gymnasien)	grammar school
der Lehrplan/Bildungsplan	curriculum
man muss .../man darf nicht ...	you must .../you must not ...
gute Noten bekommen (o-a-o)	to get good marks/grades
die Oberstufe	last 3 years of grammar school, years 10–13
die Privatschule (-n)	private school
eine Prüfung machen/bestehen	to sit/pass an exam
sich auf seine Prüfungen vorbereiten	to prepare for the exams
zur Schule/Universität gehen (*irreg*)	to go to school/university
die Schule verlassen (ä-ie-a)	to leave school
die Schulordnung	school rules
unterrichten/der Unterricht	to teach, lessons/teaching
wiederholen (*insep*)	to revise

8.1 Das Schulwesen — The school system

der Elternabend	parents' evening
die Fächerauswahl	choice of subjects
die Grundschule (-n)	primary school
die Hauptschule (-n)	secondary school (10–15)
die Realschule (-n)	secondary/technical school (10–16)
der Intensivkurs (-e)	intensive course
das Internat (-e)	boarding school
die Kernfächer (*pl*)	basic/core subjects
der Kindergarten (˜)	kindergarten, nursery school
das Leistungsfach (˜er)	main 'A' level subject
Lesen, Schreiben und Rechnen	the 3 Rs
die Nachhilfestunde (-n)	extra tuition
die Orientierungsstufe	first 2 years of secondary education
das Pflichtfach (˜er)	compulsory subject

der Realschulabschluss der Hauptschulabschluss }	secondary school leaving certificate
die allgemeine Schulpflichtzeit	(period of) compulsory schooling
sitzen bleiben* (ei-ie-ie)	to repeat a year
die Stunde (-n)	lesson
das Wahlfach (¨er)	optional subject

er wurde nicht versetzt	he has had to repeat a year
jdn. von der Schule verweisen (ei-ie-ie)	to expel s.o. from school

8.2 Lehrer und Schüler — Teachers and students

der Berufsberater (-)	careers adviser
der Externe (*adj. noun*)	day pupil
der Fachleiter (-) für (+*Acc*)	head of department of ...
der Fremdsprachenassistent (-en)	language assistant
der Hausmeister (-)	caretaker
der Hausvater (¨)/die Hausmutter (¨)	housemaster/-mistress
der Internatsschüler (-)	boarding school pupil
das Kollegium	teaching staff
der Lehrer (-)	teacher
der (Studien)referendar (-e)	student teacher (grammar school)
der Schulabgänger (-)	school-leaver
der Schuldirektor (-en)	head (of secondary school)
der Schulleiter (-)	headmaster
der Schüler (-)	pupil, school student
der Student (-en)	university student
der Tyrann (-en)	bully

8.3 Die Prüfungen — Examinations

der Abiturient (-en)	student in last year of grammar school
benoten	to mark, grade
er hat Mathe bestanden	he passed in Maths
durchfallen* (ä-ie-a)	to fail an exam
er ist durchgerutscht	he scraped through
er ist in Mathe durchgefallen	he failed in Maths
die Endnote	final mark
die Klassenarbeit (-en)	class test (continuous assessment)
eine Konkurrenzatmosphäre	a competitive atmosphere
die kontinuierliche Beurteilung	continuous assessment
der Leistungsdruck	pressure to achieve
leistungsorientiert	competitive (person, school)
mündlich, schriftlich	oral, written
eine Prüfung wiederholen (*insep*)	to retake/resit an exam
das Zeugnis (-se)	report

8.4 Der Lernprozess

The learning process

das Arbeitstier (-e)	workaholic
die Aufmerksamkeit	attentiveness
das Gedächtnis ⎫ die Gedächtniskraft ⎭	memory
ein fotografisches Gedächtnis	photographic memory
der Fehler (-)	mistake
die Gedächtnishilfe/die Eselsbrücke	memory aid/mnemonic
der Hefter (-)	file
die Legasthenie/ der Legastheniker (-)	dyslexia/dyslexic person
lernbehindert	with learning difficulties
die Lernstrategie (-n)	learning strategy
sich melden	to put up one's hand
Notizen machen	to make notes
pauken, büffeln (*inf*)	to cram
stichwortartige Notizen	outline notes
der Streber (-)	swot
das Talent (-e), die Begabung (-en)	talent, gift
sich überarbeiten (*insep*)	to overwork

**ich brauche immer eine
  Geräuschkulisse**
	I always need some background
	  noise

ohne Fleiß kein Preis	no pain, no gain (*proverb*)

8.5 Die positive Einstellung

Positive attitude

arbeiten, so gut man kann	to work to the best of one's ability
gut aufpassen	to pay attention
etw. auswendig lernen	to learn sth. by heart
ein begabter Schüler	a gifted pupil
begreifen (ei-i-i)	to grasp
sich sehr bemühen, etw. zu tun	to make every effort to do sth.
der Ehrgeiz, ehrgeizig	ambition, ambitious
die Wissenslücken stopfen	to fill in the gaps
der Wissensdurst	thirst for knowledge
sich Wissen zulegen	to acquire knowledge

sie ist den anderen haushoch überlegen	she's way ahead of the others
ich bin sehr motiviert	I'm well motivated
ich beherrsche das Wesentliche	I have a good grasp of the basics
es kostet große Mühe	it's a real effort

8.6 Die negative Einstellung   Negative attitude

abschreiben (ei-ie-ie)	to copy
sich durchwursteln *(inf)*	to muddle through
jdn. schikanieren/tyrannisieren	to bully s.o.
die Schule schwänzen	to play truant
verprügeln	to beat up

die Anstrengung lohnt sich nicht	it's not worth the effort
mit seiner Arbeit im Rückstand sein*	to be behind with one's work
einen Aufsatz hinrotzen *(inf)*	to dash off an essay
ich bin für Mathe nicht begabt	I'm not very good at Maths
das begreife ich einfach nicht	I just don't get it
ich drücke mich um die Hausaufgaben	I make excuses to get out of doing my homework
es fehlt mir an Konzentration	I lack concentration
das geht über meinen Verstand	that's beyond me
ich lerne nur auf äußeren Druck	I only learn when forced to
ich muss mir den Kopf zerbrechen	I have to rack my brains
bei einer Prüfung mogeln	to cheat in an exam
sie sitzt nach	she's in detention
er wurde von der Schule verwiesen	he was expelled from school

8.7 Der Unterricht   Teaching

abwechslungsreich	varied
wir befassen uns mit ...	we're dealing with ...
jdm. etw. beibringen *(irreg)*	to teach someone (a skill)
bestrafen	to punish
gerecht, fair	fair
jeden gleich behandeln	to treat everyone the same
Diskussionen fördern	to encourage discussion
die Disziplin aufrechterhalten (ä-ie-a)	to maintain discipline
die Disziplin straffen	to tighten up discipline
sich durchsetzen	to be assertive
konsequent	consistent
korrigieren	to mark
lasch/locker	lax/laid back
sich um ein Lehramt bewerben (i-a-o)	to apply for a teaching job
die Lehrerkonferenz (-en)	staff meeting
ein gutes Lernklima	a good atmosphere for study
der Lernstoff	material to be learned
motivieren	to motivate
Schüler/ein Fach unterrichten	to teach pupils/a subject
schwafeln *(inf)*	to waffle
unnahbar	distant, unapproachable

die Kluft zwischen Theorie und Praxis	the gap between theory and practice
er stellt hohe Ansprüche	he sets high standards
sie fesselt unser Interesse	she engages our interest
er macht einen guten Unterricht	he teaches well
eine Beziehung zu seinen Schülern finden	to relate to one's pupils
einen Schüler eine Stunde nachsitzen lassen	to give a pupil an hour's detention
sie gibt uns Unterricht in Mathe	she teaches us Maths

8.8 Das Hochschulsystem — Higher education

Altphilologie	Classics
Anglistik	English studies
das Auswahlgespräch (-e)	interview
Betriebswirtschaft	Business Studies
das Darlehen	loan
die Eignungsprüfung (-en)	aptitude test
sie hat Esprit	she's got a good brain
die Fachhochschule (-n)	tertiary technical college
die Fakultät (-en)	university faculty
Forschung betreiben (ei-ie-ie)	to do research
die Geisteswissenschaften (pl)	humanities
Germanistik	German studies
seinen Horizont erweitern	to broaden one's mind
der Hörsaal (pl Hörsäle)	lecture hall
der Hochschulabsolvent (-en) (weak noun)	graduate
die Hochschulerziehung	higher education
der Hochschullehrer (-)	university lecturer
Jura/die Rechtswissenschaft	law
die Mensa	students' refectory, canteen
die Naturwissenschaften (pl)	sciences
der Numerus clausus	restricted entry quota to university
promovieren	to do a doctorate, doctoral thesis
die Studiengebühren (pl)	tuition fees
das Studentenwohnheim (-e)	hall of residence, hostel
die Studentenbude (-n)	student digs, bedsit
der Studienabschluss (¨e)	BA/BSc
der Studienplatz (¨e)	place at university
studieren	to study, continue one's studies
ich studiere Mathe	I'm doing a Maths degree
das Studium	(programme of) studies
die Universität Bonn	University of Bonn
das Universitätsgelände (-)	campus
das Studium abbrechen (i-a-o)	to drop out of one's course

ein Studium finanzieren	to finance a course of study
eine Vorlesung halten (ä-ie-a)	to give a lecture
die ZVS	≈ UCAS (clearing house for university places)
das Abitur berechtigt zum Studium an der Universität	'A' levels give you the right to study at university
sich um einen Studienplatz bewerben (i-a-o)	to apply for a place at university
ein Fach intensiv studieren	to study a subject in depth
nach Abschluss des Studiums	after qualifying
einen akademischen Grad erhalten (ä-ie-a)	to get a degree
sie ist Dozentin für Geschichte	she lectures in history
dazu ist ein Universitätsstudium erforderlich	a degree is required for that
die gegenseitige Anerkennung von Hochschuldiplomen	mutual recognition of university degrees (in EU countries)
man kriegt BAföG für Härtefälle (pl)	people get a grant in cases of hardship
die Uni frühzeitig verlassen (ä-ie-a)	to drop out of university

8.9 Die Sonderschule   Special school

die Chancengleichheit	equality of opportunity
die Blindenschrift	braille
lernbehindert	with learning difficulties
reguläre Schulen	mainstream schools
die Zeichensprache	sign language
man nimmt auf ihre Behinderungen Rücksicht	they take account of their disabilities
man fördert die vorhandenen Fähigkeiten	they build on the abilities they have
Ausbildungschancen versäumen	to miss out on educational opportunities

8.10 Die Ausbildung   Training

die Abendschule	evening class, night school
das Abitur nachholen	to take 'A' levels later on
der Ausbildungsplatz (⁻e)	position for trainee
das Ausbildungsprogramm	training scheme
der Auszubildende (*adj. noun*) der Azubi (-s) }	trainee
berufsorientiert	work-orientated
die Berufsschule (-n)	training/F.E. college
die Einarbeitung	introductory training in company

die kaufmännische Ausbildung	business management training
die Lehre (-n)/der Lehrling (-e)	apprenticeship, training/apprentice
ein Versager sein* (irreg)	to be a failure (at school)
die Volkshochschule (-n)	adult education school
sich weiterbilden	to continue one's education/training
der zweite Bildungsweg	means of improving qualifications through night school, etc.

man sollte mehr Ausbildungsplätze zur Verfügung stellen	more training places should be made available
der Mangel an Ausbildungsplätzen	lack of traineeships

8.11 Die Bildungspolitik   Educational policy

am Arbeitsmarkt orientiert	orientated towards the job market
der Etat für Schulen	state expenditure on schools
das hat zur Folge gehabt, dass ...	the result of this has been that ...
gut ausgestattet	well-equipped
die Klassenstärke senken	to reduce class sizes
das Lehrer-Schüler-Verhältnis	the pupil–teacher ratio
die Lernmittelfreiheit	free choice of teaching materials
oben/unten auf der Prioritätenliste	high/low on the list of priorities
Reformen durchführen	to carry out reforms
das Schul- u. Wissenschafts-ministerium	Ministry of Education
sinkende Schülerzahlen	falling numbers of pupils
überfüllte Klassen	overcrowded classes
gravierende Leistungsmängel (pl)	serious underachievement
das nachlassende Leistungsniveau	falling standards (of achievement)
den Leistungsstand beurteilen	to assess achievement
die Leistungen steigern	to raise standards
den Leistungswettbewerb verstärken	to make things more competitive
Schüler zu geistiger Selbständigkeit erziehen (ie-o-o)	to educate pupils to think for themselves

eine falsche (Selbst-)Einschätzung des Leistungsvermögens	a false assessment of (one's own) abilities
die beherrschenden Themen der Bildungsdebatte	the main topics in the debate about education
die Erwartungen der Eltern erfüllen	to fulfil parental expectations
sie haben die Wahl zwischen mehreren Möglichkeiten	they have the choice of several possibilities
je nach Neigungen und Fähigkeiten	according to interests and abilities
es muss vorrangig behandelt werden	it must be given top priority

sie laden ihre Aggression in der Schule ab	they vent their aggression in school
leistungsstarke Schüler sollten verstärkt gefördert werden	able pupils should be stretched

Das Schulsystem
http://www.bmbf.de/ *Bundesministerium für Bildung und Forschung*
http://www.bildungsserver.de/ *Deutscher Bildungsserver*
http://portal.bildung.hessen.de/ *Bildungsserver Hessen*
http://www.bildung.at/ *das Bildungsportal in Österreich*
http://www.sbf.admin.ch *Bildung und Forschung (Schweiz)*

Die Prüfungen
http://www.abitur.de/ *Abitur in Deutschland*
http://www.g8-in-bayern.de *Achtjähriges Gymnasium in Bayern*

Die Schüler
http://www.schueler-union.de/ *Schüler Union Deutschlands*
http://www.jugend-forscht.de/ *Stiftung Jugend forscht e.V.*

Die Lehrer
http://www.lehrer-werden.de/ *Lehrer werden*

Die Ausbildung
http://www.ausbildung-plus.de/ *Berufsausbildung*
http://www.ihk-ausbildung.de/ *Ausbildungsplätze 2006*
http://www.azubitage.de/ *Messe für Ausbildung und Studium*
http://www.jaau.nrw.de/ *Jugend, Arbeit und Ausbildung*
http://www.bibb.de *Bundesinstitut für Berufsbildung*

Die Bildungspolitik
http://www.kmk.org *Kultusministerkonferenz KMK Bonn*
http://www.bmbwk.gv.at/ *Bildung, Wissenschaft, Kultur (Österreich)*

Das Hochschulsystem
http://www.campus-germany.de/ *Studieren in Deutschland*
www.studieren.de *Infos zum Studium*
http://www.studieren.at *Studieren in Österreich*
http://www.studentenwerke.de/ *Deutsches Studentenwerk*

Verschiedenes
http://www.alphabetisierung.de/ *Alphabetisierung und Grundbildung*
http://www.daad.de *DAAD – Deutscher Akademischer Austauschdienst*
http://www.schulweb.de/ *Schulen, Schulmaterialien, Schüleraustausch*
www.san-ev.de *Schulen ans Netz e.V.*
http://www.schulen-ans-netz.de/ *Schulen im Internet*

9 Stadt- und Landleben

Die Stadt	The town
die Altstadt (⁼e)	old part of town
das Einkaufszentrum (-zentren)	shopping centre
der Einwohner (-)	inhabitant
die Fabrik (-en)	factory
die Fußgängerzone (-n)	pedestrian zone
das Gebäude (-)	building
die Gegend (-en)	area, vicinity, neighbourhood
die Großstadt (⁼e)	city, large town
die Heimat	home town, native country
die Hauptverkehrszeit	rush hour
das Industriegebiet (-e)	industrial area
das Kaufhaus (⁼er)	department store
modern; alt; laut; belebt; lebendig	modern; old; noisy; busy; lively
parken	to park
das Parkhaus (⁼er)	multi-storey car park
der Parkplatz (⁼e)	car park, parking lot
pendeln/der Pendler	to commute/commuter
die Stadtmitte, die Innenstadt ⎫ das Stadtzentrum (-zentren) ⎭	town centre
der Vorort (-e)	suburb
die Wohnung (-en)	flat, apartment, home

9.1 Die Stadt — The town

das Armenviertel (-)	slum
das Ballungsgebiet (-e)	conurbation
ein bebautes Gebiet	a built-up area
die Behörde (-n) ⎫ die Verwaltung (-en) ⎭	administration, authorities
der Bürger (-)	citizen
die Grünanlagen (pl)	green spaces, parks
die Infrastruktur	infrastructure
das kulturelle Leben	cultural life
der Nachbar (-n)	neighbour
das Notstandsgebiet (-e)	depressed area
die Schlafstadt (⁼e)	dormitory town
am Stadtrand	on the edge of town
die Stadt Stuttgart	city of Stuttgart

der Stadtbewohner (-)	town dweller
die Stuttgarter (*invar*) Kirchen	Stuttgart's churches
die städtische Bevölkerung	the urban population
die städtische Lebensweise	city way of life
von ... umgeben	surrounded by ...
zentral gelegen	situated in the town centre
ein breites Freizeitangebot machen	to offer a wide range of leisure activities

9.2 Die Stadtplanung — Town planning

abreißen (ei-i-i)	to demolish
baufällig	dilapidated, unsafe
der Bauplatz im Grünen	greenfield development site
die Baustelle (-n)	building site
der Bedarf an Bauland	the need for building land
der Beton	concrete
die Busspur (-en)	bus lane
einstürzen*	to fall down
das Grundstück (-e)	building plot
das Hochhaus (¨er)	tall building, skyscraper
das Lagerhaus (¨er)	warehouse
leer stehen (*irreg*)	to stand empty
modernisieren	to modernise
die Passage (-n)	shopping arcade
sanieren	to renovate, redevelop
die Sanierung	redevelopment, renovation
der Städtebau	urban development
das Stadtviertel (-)	district
etw. steuerlich fördern	to give tax incentives for sth.
die Straßenbeleuchtung	street lighting
umbauen (zu +*Dat*)	to convert building (to), to renovate
die Verkehrsader (-n)	main road, arterial road
vernachlässigen	to neglect
verschönern	to beautify
die Vorstadt (¨e)	suburbs
das Wohngebiet (-e)	housing area
die Wohnsiedlung (-en)	housing estate
das Wohnungsbauprogramm	housing programme
die Zentrale (-n)	head office

9.3 Wohnungen — Housing

ausziehen, umziehen (ie-o-o)	to move out, to move house
bei mir/zu mir	at my house/to my house
besitzen (i-a-e)	to own
die Eigentumswohnung (-en)	owner-occupied flat

das Einzelhaus (⁼er)	detached house
Gas, Heizung, Strom	gas, heating, electricity
geräumig	roomy
der Hauseigentümer (-) ⎫ der Wohnungseigentümer ⎭	home owner
die Hypothekenzinsen (*pl*)	mortgage rates
der Immobilienmakler (-)	estate agent, realtor
instand setzen	to repair
instand halten (ä-ie-a)	to maintain
die Kommunalsteuer	council tax
die Miete (-n)/der Mieter (-)	rent/tenant
das möblierte Zimmer (-)	bedsit
die Nebenkosten (*pl*)	outgoings (on fuel, etc.)
putzen	to clean
das Reihenhaus (⁼er)	terraced house
die Sozialwohnung (-en)	council flat
teilen	to share
der Vermieter (-)	landlord
vorfertigen	to prefabricate
wohnlich	homely, cosy
der Wohnblock (⁼e)	block of flats
die Wohngemeinschaft (-en)	people sharing house
der Wohnungsbedarf	housing needs
der Wohnungsmangel ⎫ die Wohnungsnot ⎭	housing shortage
das Wohnsilo (-s) (*pej*)	rabbit hutches (*pej*)
die Wohnverhältnisse (*pl*)	living conditions
eine Zweizimmerwohnung	flat with two rooms (excl. kitchen, bathroom)
die Zimmervermittlung	accommodation agency

9.4 Probleme des Stadtlebens Problems of living in town

die Anonymität	anonymity
die Armut	poverty
die Barackensiedlung, (-stadt)	shanty town
benachteiligt	deprived
der Berufsverkehr	commuter/rush hour traffic
die Betonwüste	concrete jungle
betteln	to beg
der Bettler (-)	beggar
die Einsamkeit	loneliness
das Elendsviertel (-)	slums, sink estate
die Gesellschaft	company (of other people)
der Härtefall (⁼e)	case of hardship
die Hektik, das Gedränge	hustle and bustle
obdachlos	homeless

das Ödland	wasteland
schnorren (inf)	to scrounge
der Stop-and-go-Verkehr	bumper-to-bumper traffic
der Straßenraub	mugging (category of crime)
der Überfall (¨e)	mugging (incident)
der Stadtstreicher (-)	vagrant
die Stadtstreicherei	vagrancy
die Verschmutzung	pollution
die Stadtflucht	exodus from the cities
ohne festen Wohnsitz	of no fixed abode
die Bodenpreise schnellen* in die Höhe	land prices are going through the roof
im Freien übernachten	to sleep rough
von der Hand in den Mund leben	to live from hand to mouth
von zu Hause weglaufen	to run away from home
der Trend zu Einpersonenhaushalten	the trend towards single-person households

Das Land Country

abgelegen	remote
anbauen (tr)	to grow sth.
der Bauer (-n)/die Bäuerin (-nen) } der Landwirt (-e)	farmer
der Bauernhof (¨e)	farm
der Berg (-e); in den Bergen	mountain; in the mountains
bergig	mountainous
die Ernte	crop, produce
das Feld (-er)	field
die Ferienwohnung (-en)	holiday flat/house
der Fluss (¨e)	river
die frische Luft	fresh air
im Grünen	in the country
die Küste; an der Küste	coast; on the coast
das Land; auf dem Land	the country(-side); in the country
leblos	lifeless
die Landschaft	landscape
die Landwirtschaft	agriculture
malerisch	picturesque
die Natur	nature
ruhig	quiet
der Wald (¨er)	wood, forest

9.5 Auf dem Land leben | Living in the country

das Erholungsgebiet	holiday/recreation area
unberührte Natur erleben	to enjoy unspoiled countryside
die Bucht (-en)	bay
geruhsam	peaceful, leisurely
die Landflucht	rural depopulation
wo sich Fuchs und Hase „Gute Nacht" sagen	in the sticks/the back of beyond
man ist aufs Auto angewiesen	people are dependent on the car
die Strukturschwäche in ländlichen Gebieten	rural deprivation

9.6 Die Landwirtschaft | Agriculture

anbauen	to cultivate, grow
das Bauerndorf (-̈er)	farming community
erben	to inherit
ernten	to harvest
die Ernte (-n)	harvest, crop
die Forstwirtschaft	forestry
das Getreide	cereal crops
der Getreideanbau	arable farming
der Großbetrieb (-e)	large farm
der Kleinbauer (-n)/ die Kleinbäuerin (-nen)	smallholder
der Landbewohner (-)	country dweller
der Mähdrescher (-)	combine harvester
pflügen	to plough
die Milchviehhaltung	dairy farming
der Rinderwahnsinn	mad cow disease, BSE
säen	to sow
der Weizen	wheat
das Feld (-er)/die Wiese (-n)	field/meadow
der Winzer (-)/der Weinbauer (-n)	wine-grower
der Weinberg (-e)	vineyard
die Weinlese (-n)	grape harvest
wiederaufforsten	to reforest
das Wild	game
Bäume einschlagen/fällen	to fell trees
den Wald roden	to clear forest land
staatliche Hilfen	state subsidies
die Massentierhaltung	intensive livestock farming

eine Übertragung des Rinderwahnsinns auf den Menschen kann nicht ausgeschlossen werden	the transmission of mad cow disease to humans cannot be ruled out
die künstlichen Düngemittel	artificial fertilisers

9.7 Die Zukunft der Landwirtschaft — The future of agriculture

der Bio-Landwirtschaftsbetrieb (-e)	organic farm
diversifizieren	to diversify
die Legebatterie (-n)	battery farm
leistungsfähig	efficient
der Ökobauer (-n)/die Ökobäuerin (-nen)	organic farmer
der Pächter (-)	tenant farmer
rentabel	economic
verpachten	to lease out
die zunehmende Mechanisierung	increasing mechanisation
die industriell betriebene Viehzucht	factory farming
die Gemeinsame Agrarpolitik	Common Agricultural Policy (CAP)
die Quoten (*pl*) für die Milcherzeugung	milk production quotas
die Nahrungsmittelproduktion	food production
die Überschussproduktion drosseln	to cut back surplus production
aus der landwirtschaftlichen Nutzung herausnehmen (i-a-o)	to set aside (from agricultural use)
die Flächenstilllegung	'setting aside' agricultural land
das Land ökologisch bewirtschaften	to farm organically

Die Stadtplanung
http://www.virtuelle-stadtplanung.de   *virtuelle Stadtplanung online*

Wohnungen
http://www.wowi.de/   *das wohnungswirtschaftliche Forum im Netz*

Die Landwirtschaft
http://www.landwirtschaft.ch/   *Schweizer Landwirtschaft*
www.bmelv.de   *Landwirtschaft*
www.cma.de   *Deutsches Essen*

Verschiedenes
http://www.bib-demographie.de/   *Bundesinstitut für Bevölkerungsforschung*

10 Die Arbeitswelt

anstellen/einstellen	to employ
der/die Angestellte (*adj. noun*)	employee
sie arbeitet bei ...	she works for ...
arbeitslos	unemployed
das Arbeitsamt/die Arbeitsangentur	job centre
die Ausbildung	training
der Beamte (*adj. noun*)/	civil servant, government employee
die Beamtin (-nen)	
der Beruf (-e)	occupation, profession
die Berufsberatung	careers advice
berufstätig	working, having a job
das Berufspraktikum	work experience
der Betrieb	business, concern
der Feierabend	closing time (and the time after it)
das Gehalt ($^-$er)	salary
der Geschäftsmann ($^-$er)/	businessman/-woman
die Geschäftsfrau (-en)	
die Geschäftszeiten	business hours
gut bezahlt	well paid
hoch qualifiziert	well qualified
die Karriere (-n)	career
eine Stelle suchen	to look for a job
die Teilzeitarbeit	part-time work
verdienen	to earn
der Verkäufer (-)	salesperson, shop assistant
der Wirtschaftsprüfer	accountant
Zeitungen austragen (ä-u-a)	to deliver newspapers

10.1 Eine Stelle suchen   Looking for a job

die Annonce (-n)	advertisement
die Arbeitsmarktlage	state of the job market
sich in (*+Dat*) ... auskennen	to have to know about ...
müssen	
ein begehrter Posten	a much sought-after job
die Berufsaussichten	career prospects
sich bewerben um (*+Acc*) (i-a-o)	to apply for
die Branche (-n)	area of business, trade, industry
der Berufsberater (-)	careers adviser
die Berufswahl	choice of career

ehrgeizig/der Ehrgeiz	ambitious/ambition
die Eigenschaft (-en)	(personal) characteristic
eine Firma direkt anschreiben (ei-ie-ie)	to write to a firm direct
jdn. um Rat fragen	to ask s.o. for advice
im Sprachen-/Finanzbereich	in the field of languages/finance
eine passende Stelle	a suitable job
eine freie Stelle	vacancy
die Stellenangebote (pl)	situations vacant
unterqualifiziert sein* (irreg)	to be under-qualified
die Stellenvermittlung (-en)	employment agency

beruflich erfolgreich sein	to be successful in one's career
was sind Sie von Beruf?	what do you do for a living?
innerbetriebliche Ausbildung	on-the-job training
mir stehen viele Berufe offen	I have a wide range of career possibilities

das erfordert Ihre Eigeninitiative	you have to use your own initiative
ich möchte einen Beruf in Richtung Elektronik ergreifen	I'd like to go for a career that has something to do with electronics
sich den Anzeigenteil der Zeitung ansehen	to look at the advertisements in the newspaper
welche Anforderungen werden an die Ausbildung gestellt?	what are the requirements in terms of training?

10.2 Die Bewerbung — The application

etw. beilegen	to enclose sth. (with a letter)
die Berufserfahrung	experience (professional)
das Bewerbungsschreiben (-)	letter (of application)
das Foto (-s)/das Lichtbild (-er)	photograph
die Fotokopie (-n)	photocopy
gute Kenntnisse in …	a good knowledge of …
der Lebenslauf	curriculum vitæ, CV
sehr motiviert	well motivated
persönliche Daten (pl)	personal details
die Qualifikationen (pl)	qualifications
die Referenz (-en)	referee, reference
die Unterlagen (pl)	documents

das Bewerbungsformular ausfüllen	to fill in an application form
sich bewerben um eine Stelle als …	to apply for a job as …
jdm. als Referenz dienen	to be a referee for s.o.
Deutschkenntnisse erforderlich	a knowledge of German required
ich kann fließend Deutsch	I can speak fluent German
jdn. als Referenz angeben (i-a-e)	to give s.o. as a referee
seine EDV-Kenntnisse ausnutzen	to use one's knowledge of computers

10.3 Das Vorstellungsgespräch Interview

jdm. eine Absage erteilen	to turn s.o. down
der Arbeitsvertrag (⁼e)	job contract
der gesicherte Arbeitsplatz (⁼e)	job security
die Aufgabe (-n)	task
einen guten Eindruck machen	to make a good impression
der Gesprächspartner (-)	interviewer
dezente Kleidung tragen (ä-u-a)	to dress well
gepflegt	well-groomed
sich hocharbeiten	to work one's way up
Testverfahren einsetzen	to use tests
gute Umgangsformen	good manners
die Verdienstmöglichkeiten	earnings potential
einen Vertrag unterschreiben (ei-ie-ie)	to sign a contract
jdn. zum Vorstellungsgespräch einladen (ä-u-a)	to invite s.o. for interview
die Zusage (-n)	(firm) job offer

man hat mir die Stelle angeboten	they offered me the job
wie sehen die Aufstiegsmöglichkeiten aus?	what are the career prospects?
es ist ein Schritt nach vorn	it's a step up the ladder
Sie bekommen einen schriftlichen Bescheid	you will receive notification in writing
wie verhalten Sie sich in einer Stress-Situation?	how do you react in stressful situations?
man will ermitteln, ob ein Bewerber der Stelle gewachsen ist	they want to find out whether an applicant is suitable for the job
ist der Test ausschlaggebend?	is the test decisive?
Geschick im Umgang mit Menschen haben **geschickt mit Menschen umgehen können** ⎫⎬⎭	to be good at dealing with people

10.4 Die Geschäftsorganisation Business organisation

die Abteilung (-en)	department
die Abwesenheitsquote	the rate of absenteeism
der Arbeitgeber (-)	employer
der Arbeitnehmer (-)	employee
die Arbeitskräfte (*pl*) ⎫ die Belegschaft ⎭	workforce, manpower
am Arbeitsplatz	at work, in the office
im Aufsichtsrat sitzen (*irreg*)	to be on the board of directors
der/die Aufsichtsratsvorsitzende (*adj. noun*)	chairman/-woman of the board
das Bankwesen	banking
das Baugewerbe	construction industry
beschäftigen	to employ
der Betriebsleiter (-)	works manager
der Buchhalter (-)	accountant
die Dienstleistungen (*pl*)	service industries
die Erwerbstätigen (*pl*)	the working population
die Fabrik (-en)	factory
im Geschäft sein (*irreg*)	to be in business
der Geschäftsführer (-)	managing director, CEO
die Geschäftsstelle (-n), die Filiale (-n)	branch
das Gewerbe (-)	trade
das Hotelgewerbe	hotel trade
der Meister (-)/die Meisterin (-nen)	master craftsman/-woman
die Mitbestimmung	co-determination/worker participation in management
der öffentliche Dienst	civil service
das Personal	personnel, staff
der Personalleiter (-)	personnel manager
die Publicrelations/Public Relations	public relations
die Sitzung (-en), die Besprechung (-en)	meeting
die Konferenz (-en)	meeting, conference
der Unternehmer (-)	entrepreneur, employer
der Verkaufsleiter (-)	sales manager
der Verlag (-e)	publishing company
der Vorarbeiter (-)	foreman
der/die Vorgesetzte (*adj. noun*)	superior
der/die Vorsitzende (*adj. noun*)	chairperson
die Werbeagentur (-en)	advertising agency
die Zentrale (-n)	head office
die Zusammenarbeit	cooperation
leistungsorientiert arbeiten	to aim for efficiency

10.5 Der Arbeitnehmer   The employee

sie arbeitet bei Daimler-Benz	she works for Mercedes-Benz
arbeitsscheu	work shy
der Arbeitstag (-e)	working day
das Arbeitstier (-e)	workaholic
der/die Auszubildende (*adj. noun*)	trainee
befördert werden (*irreg*)	to gain promotion
belebt, geschäftig	busy (lively)
beschäftigt	busy (a lot to do)
der Drückeberger (-)	shirker
durch Erfahrung lernen	to learn by experience
der Geschäftssinn	business sense, acumen
der Lehrling (-e)	apprentice
schwarzarbeiten	to work illegally
verantwortlich/zuständig	responsible
pendeln/der Pendler (-)	to commute/commuter
der Termin (-e)	appointment, deadline
der Techniker (-)	technician
der Vertreter (-)	representative
die Zeitarbeit	temporary work

auf dem Weg nach oben sein	to be on the way up
in eine leitende Stellung aufrücken	to reach a top position
er hat es aus eigener Kraft zum Millionär gebracht	he's a self-made millionaire
der ständige Konkurrenzkampf	rat race
der steigende Leistungsdruck	increasing pressure to achieve
die Zufriedenheit am Arbeitsplatz	job satisfaction

10.6 Die Arbeitsbedingungen   Working conditions

die Arbeitsplatzteilung	job-sharing
aufhören zu arbeiten	to retire
als Aushilfssekretär(in) arbeiten	to temp
die Beförderung	promotion
die dynamische Rente	index-linked pension
der Elternurlaub	paternity/maternity leave
der Feierabend	end of work (for the day)
der Feiertag (-e)	day off, holiday
freiberuflich	self-employed
die Ganztagsarbeit	full-time work
die Gelegenheitsarbeit	casual work
die gleitende Arbeitszeit	flexible working hours, flexitime
der Kollege (-n)/die Kollegin (-nen) der Mitarbeiter (-) }	colleague

das Mobbing	bullying/harassment
im Pensionsalter	of retirement age
die Probezeit	probationary period
der Rentner (-)	pensioner
die Schichtarbeit	shift work
selbständig arbeiten	to be self-employed
die Spesen (*pl*)	business expenses
eine stumpfsinnige Arbeit	boring work/job
er arbeitet Teilzeit	he works part time
die Telearbeit	teleworking, working from home
Überstunden machen	to do overtime
der Urlaub	holiday

heute war viel los	it was a busy day today
eine wöchentliche Arbeitszeit von 35 Stunden	a 35-hour working week
eine verantwortungsvolle Stelle	a responsible job
außerhalb der normalen Arbeitszeiten arbeiten	to work unsocial hours

10.7 Die Arbeitslosigkeit   Unemployment

der ungelernte Arbeiter	unskilled worker
der angelernte Arbeiter	semi-skilled worker
der gelernte Arbeiter ⎫ der Facharbeiter ⎭	skilled worker
arbeitslos/die Arbeitslosigkeit	unemployed/unemployment
sich arbeitslos melden	to register as unemployed
die Arbeitslosenhilfe ⎫ das Arbeitslosengeld ⎭	unemployment benefit, dole
eine Arbeitslosenrate von 6 %	an unemployment rate of 6%
der Arbeitsplatzabbau	job cuts
die Armut	poverty
die Dunkelziffer	estimated number of unreported cases

entlassen (ä-ie-a), feuern	to sack, dismiss
fristlos	without notice
die Frustration (-en)	frustration
die Kündigung (-en)	notice of dismissal
der Kündigungsschutz	protection against (wrongful) dismissal
die Langzeitarbeitslosen	long-term unemployed
die natürliche Personalreduzierung	natural wastage
der Rationalisierungsschub	the drive to rationalise (working practices)

rausfliegen (*inf*)	to get the sack
die Selbstachtung	self-respect, self-esteem
überhöhte Lohnkosten	excessive wage costs

bestimmte Arbeitsplätze überflüssig machen	to make certain jobs superfluous
Arbeitsplätze gingen verloren	jobs were lost
Arbeitskräfte einsparen	to cut back on jobs
sie haben das Gefühl, nicht gebraucht zu werden	they have the feeling that they are not needed
es schlägt leicht in Apathie um	it easily turns into apathy
100 Angestellte wurden entlassen	100 employees lost their jobs
die Arbeitslosenzahlen steigen monatlich	the unemployment figures are rising month after month
betroffen sind vor allem ...	those most affected are ...
er ist auf Sozialhilfe angewiesen	he's dependent on state hand-outs
man hat die ganze Belegschaft Feierschichten machen lassen	they laid off the entire workforce
sie geraten in finanzielle Schwierigkeiten	they are getting into financial difficulties
vorzeitig in den Ruhestand gehen* (*irreg*)	to take early retirement

10.8 Neue Arbeitsplätze   New jobs

die Arbeitsbeschaffungsmaßnahmen (*pl*), ABM	job creation schemes
flexibel	adaptable, flexible
freie Arbeitsplätze	vacancies
Gegenmaßnahmen ergreifen	to take counter-measures
die neuen Technologien (*pl*)	new technologies
die Umschulung	retraining
neue Arbeitsplätze wurden geschaffen	new jobs were created
Maßnahmen zum Abbau der Arbeitslosigkeit	measures to reduce unemployment
der Einsatz neuer Techniken	the introduction of new technologies
der Computer funktioniert reibungslos	the computer works efficiently
sich den veränderten Verhältnissen anpassen	to adapt to change
die Produktion auf computergestützte Fertigung umstellen	to switch production to computerised methods
mit dem technischen Wandel zurechtkommen	to cope with technological change
der Mangel an qualifizierten Arbeitskräften	shortage of qualified staff

10.9 Frauen im Beruf   Women at work

die Frauenquote	proportion of jobs set for women
die Gleichberechtigung	equal rights
das Kindergeld	family allowance
die Kinderkrippe (-n)	creche, nursery
die sexuelle Belästigung	sexual harassment
sich verwirklichen	to fulfil oneself

gleicher Lohn für gleiche Arbeit — equal pay for equal work
wenn Frauen gleichwertige Arbeit wie Männer verrichten, dann sollten sie ... — if women do work equal in value to men's, they should ...
wie bewertet man die Arbeit? — how do you assess the value of the work?
Frauen sind Benachteiligungen ausgesetzt — women are subjected to discrimination
Schutzvorschriften für Schwangere — regulations to protect pregnant women
der Anteil von Frauen in führenden Positionen im Wirtschaftsleben — the proportion of women in top executive positions
mehr Frauen mit Familie wollen zurück in den Beruf — more women with families want to go back to their careers
ein Prozess des Umdenkens — a rethinking process

10.10 Die Gewerkschaften   Trade unions

die Arbeitskampfmaßnahmen (*pl*)	industrial action
die Arbeitsstreitigkeit (-en)	industrial dispute
die Arbeitszeitverkürzung (-en)	reduction in working hours
die Aussperrung	lock-out
der Bummelstreik/Dienst nach Vorschrift	go-slow
eine Fabrik bestreiken	to black/go on strike at a factory
die Forderungen nach (+*Dat*)	demands for
die Gewerkschaft (-en)	trade union
der Gewerkschaftler (-)	trade unionist
höhere Löhne fordern	to demand higher wages
der Lohnstopp	pay freeze
die Schlichtungsverhandlungen (*pl*)	strike settlement negotiations
die Tarifverhandlungen	pay negotiations
der Tarifvertrag (⁻e)	pay agreement
der Vertrauensmann (⁻er)	shop steward

der Schlichtungsversuch scheiterte	the attempt at arbitration broke down
einen Streik ausrufen (u-ie-u)	to call a strike
in den Streik treten* (i-a-e)	to go on strike
industrielle Arbeitsbeziehungen (*pl*)	industrial relations
die Tarife für Löhne kündigen	to put in a wage claim
ein vollorganisiertes Unternehmen	closed shop
wild streiken	to be on unofficial strike
einen neutralen Schlichter einbeziehen (ie-o-o)	to call in an independent arbitrator
die Verlängerung des Urlaubs	lengthening the holiday
man hat vor der Fabrik Streikposten aufgestellt	they picketed the factory
die Kosten des Streiks werden auf ... beziffert	the cost of the strike is estimated at ...

Eine Stelle suchen

http://www.arbeitsagentur.de/ *Bundesagentur für Arbeit*

http://www.arbeit-online.de/ *Stellenangebote*

http://www.minijob-zentrale.de/ *Informationsstelle der Bundesknappschaft*

http://www.bewerbung-tipps.com/ *Tipps für das Anschreiben einer Bewerbung*

Die Arbeit

http://www.schader-stiftung.de/wohn_wandel/357.php *Wandel der Arbeitswelt*

http://www.arbeitsrecht.org *Arbeitsrecht*

http://www.frau-und-beruf-sh.de/ *Frau und Beruf Schleswig-Holstein*

Die Arbeitslosigkeit

http://www.schader-stiftung.de/gesellschaft_wandel/441.php *Arbeitslosigkeit*

http://www.erwerbslose.de/ *Deutschlands umfangreichstes Arbeitslosen-Portal*

Die Gewerkschaften

http://www.verdi.de/ *Vereinte Dienstleistungsgewerkschaft*

http://www.dgb.de/ *Deutscher Gewerkschaftsbund*

Verschiedenes

http://www.bmas.bund.de/ *Bundesministerium für Arbeit und Soziales*

www.arbeitsamt.de *Weiterleitung zur Bundesagentur für Arbeit*

http://www.infoquelle.de/ *Online-Wirtschaftsmagazin*

http://iab.de/ *Institut für Arbeitsmarkt- und Berufsforschung*

11 Wirtschaft und Geschäft

Angebot und Nachfrage	supply and demand
die Dienstleistungen (pl)	service industries
die Einkommenssteuer	income tax
die Fabrik (-en)	factory
die Firma (pl Firmen)	firm, company
der Gewinn (-e)	profit
herstellen, erzeugen	to make, produce, manufacture
der Hersteller (-)	manufacturer
der Import/Export	import/export
importieren/exportieren	to import/export
die Inflation	inflation
der Kapitalismus	capitalism
die Konkurrenz, konkurrenzfähig	competition, competitive
der Kunde (-n)	customer
die Massenproduktion	mass production
die Rezession	recession
der Staat	the state
der Termin (-e)	appointment, deadline
der Verlust (-e)	loss
die Währung	currency
der Zinssatz	interest rate

11.1 Grundbegriffe — Basic terminology

der Aktionär (-e)	shareholder
die Bezahlung (-en)	payment
der Einzelhandel	retail trade
der Existenzgründer (-)	entrepreneur
fähig (person); leistungsfähig (machine)	efficient
Gewinn erzielen	to make profit (person)
der Großhandel	wholesale trade
Hoch- und Tiefbau	structural and civil engineering
die Landwirtschaft	agriculture
der Maschinenbau	mechanical engineering
die Steuer (-n)	tax
der Umsatz	turnover
der Verbraucher (-)	consumer
die Verbrauchergesellschaft	consumer society
der Volkswirt	economist
das Wirtschaftswachstum	economic growth

die Wohlstandsgesellschaft	affluent society
die Zahlungsbilanz	balance of payments
Zulieferer und Abnehmer	suppliers and customers
die freie Marktwirtschaft	free market economy
die soziale Marktwirtschaft	social market economy

11.2 Die Wirtschaftspolitik   Economic policy

die Aussichten (*pl*)	prospects
das Bruttosozialprodukt	gross national product (GNP)
das Defizit	deficit
die Flaute (-n) (*inf*)	(economic) depression
der Haushaltsplan	budget
die Hochkonjunktur ⎫ der Aufschwung ⎭	boom, upturn
die Ich-AG	one-person business
die Konjunktur	economic situation
die Lebenshaltungskosten (*pl*)	cost of living
der Lebenshaltungskostenindex	cost-of-living index
der Leitzins	base rate
der Mini-Job (-s)	low-paid part-time job
die Preise erhöhen/herabsetzen	to raise/lower prices
privatisieren	to privatise
die Strategie (-n)	strategy
die Subvention (-en)	subsidy
subventionieren	to subsidise
verstaatlichen	to nationalise
die Wirtschaftslage	economic situation
die Wirtschaft ankurbeln	to boost the economy
das Wirtschaftsministerium	Department of Trade and Industry
das Wirtschaftswunder	German post-war economic recovery
der Zinsanstieg	rise in interest rates
eine ansteigende/rückläufige Tendenz	upward/downward trend
der öffentliche/private Sektor	public/private sector
die Produktion durch Subventionen fördern	to encourage production by means of subsidies
in eine Krise geraten (ä-ie-a)*	to go into crisis
den Etat auf dem Vorjahresstand einfrieren	to freeze the budget at the same level as the previous year
etw. auf eine solide Grundlage stellen	to put sth. onto a firm footing
die Preise steigen*/sinken*/ schnellen* in die Höhe	prices are rising/falling/shooting up

eine nachhaltige Verbesserung	a sustained recovery
wir stehen vor erheblichen Problemen	we face considerable problems
wirtschaftspolitisch sollte man ...	as far as economic policy is concerned, they ought to ...
die Inflation bekämpfen	to fight inflation
die Bekämpfung der Inflation	the fight against inflation
die Voraussetzung für die Lösung aller wirtschaftlichen Probleme	the precondition for solving all economic problems
die Inflation ist zurückgegangen	inflation has fallen
die Zinssätze erhöhen	to raise interest rates
der gesetzliche Mindestlohn	statutory minimum wage
überhöhte Lohnkosten	excessive wage costs
die Arbeitslosigkeit	unemployment
eine Arbeitslosenrate von 6 %	an unemployment rate of 6%

11.3 Das Steuerwesen — Taxation

brutto/netto	before/after tax, gross/net
das Finanzamt	Inland Revenue
die Mehrwertsteuer (MwSt)	value added tax (VAT)
die Steuereinnahmen (pl)	revenue from taxation
die Steuerlast	tax burden
das Steuerparadies	tax haven
die Steuern herabsetzen/ erhöhen	to lower/raise taxes
etw. mit Steuergeldern finanzieren	to finance sth. from taxpayers' money

11.4 Die Firma — The company

das Angebot	goods on offer/produced
der Auftrag (¨e) die Bestellung (-en)	order
der Aufsichtsrat	board
der Besitzer (-)	owner
der Betrieb (-e)	firm, company, factory
der Chef (-s)	head, boss
der Dienstleistungsbetrieb (-e)	service industry
der Direktor (-en)	director
die Firma (pl Firmen) das Geschäft (-e) die Gesellschaft (-en) das Unternehmen (-)	firm, company
der Jahresumsatz	annual turnover
die Konkurrenzfähigkeit	competitiveness
das Lager(-haus)	warehouse

die Lieferung (-en)	delivery
der Lieferant (-en)	supplier
der (Abteilungs-)Leiter (-) ⎫	
der Manager (-) ⎭	(departmental) manager
der multinationale Konzern (-e)	multinational company
die Produktivität pro Kopf	output per head
sich selbständig machen	to go into business
die Sparte (-n)	line of business
der Sprecher (-)	spokesperson
die Transportkosten (*pl*)	transport costs
die Versicherung	insurance
der Vertreter (-)	rep, salesperson
vorrätig haben/sein	to have/be in stock
die Waren (*pl*)	goods
die Wartung	maintenance, servicing

die Firma wurde 1950 gegründet	the firm was founded in 1950
er leitet die Filiale in Dresden	he manages the branch in Dresden
Produktionsprozesse automatisieren	to automate production
mit jdm. ein Geschäft gründen	to go into business with s.o.
am Fließband arbeiten	to work on the assembly line
die Produktion ins Ausland verlagern	to transfer production abroad

11.5 Der Geschäftsalltag   Everyday business life

die Anfrage	enquiry
einer Anzeige folgen	to respond to an advertisement
ein Auto mieten	to hire a car
jdm. Bescheid sagen	to let s.o. know
sich beschweren bei jdm.	to complain to
die Beschwerde (-n)	complaint
die Dienstreise (-n)	business trip
sich erkundigen nach (+*Dat*)	to make an enquiry about
der Flug (¨-e)	flight
eine Frist einhalten (ä-ie-a)	to keep to a deadline
um Informationen über ... bitten (i-a-e)	to request information on ...
der Kostenvoranschlag	estimate of costs
der Kundendienst	after-sales service
der Dienst am Kunden	customer service
die Mahnung (-en)	reminder
die Rechnung (-en)	invoice
die Mitteilung (-en)	memo, report
das Protokoll/protokollieren	minutes/to take minutes
das Publicity-/Werbematerial	publicity materials
die Reservierung	booking
der Schaden/beschädigen	damage/to damage
stornieren/die Stornierung	to cancel/cancellation (reservation, order)

die Tagesordnung	agenda
der Treffpunkt	venue
die Unterkunft	accommodation
die Verspätung	delay
die Verzögerung	delay
vorgesehen/geplant	scheduled
zusammenfassen	to summarise

einen Termin einhalten (ä-ie-a)	to meet a deadline, keep an appointment
mit einer Beschwerde fertig werden*	to deal with a complaint
die Konferenz musste abgesagt werden	the conference had to be cancelled
wir weisen darauf hin, dass ...	we wish to remind you that ...
einen Termin mit jdm. vereinbaren	to make an appointment with s.o.
für etw./jdn. Vorbereitungen treffen	to make arrangements for sth./s.o.
eine Besprechung/Konferenz/ Ausstellung organisieren	to organise a meeting/ conference/exhibition
die Versicherung kommt dafür auf	the insurance company pays for it

11.6 Angebot und Nachfrage   Supply and demand

der Großeinkauf	bulk purchase
der Konkurrent (-en)	competitor
die Marke (-n)	make, brand name
das Marketing	marketing
marktbestimmt	market-led (e.g. decision)
der Marktanteil (-e)	market share
der Marktführer (-)	market leader
ein Produkt vermarkten	to market a product
für ein Produkt werben (i-a-o)	to promote a product
der Prozentsatz	percentage
5 Prozent Rabatt	a 5% discount
eine fünfprozentige Erhöhung	a 5% increase
der Schaden/beschädigen	damage/to damage
der Schlussverkauf	sale, end-of-season sale
das Sonderangebot	special offer
die Verkaufsziffern (*pl*)	sales figures
die Verzögerung (-en)	delay
der Vorreiter sein	to be the first on the market

es herrscht eine starke Nachfrage nach ...	there is a great demand for ...
Nachfrage erzeugen	to create a market
auf dem Markt erscheinen	to come on to the market
den Markt überschwemmen	to flood the market

ein Markt mit starker Konkurrenz	a highly competitive market
das Produkt muss mit billigeren konkurrieren	this product has to compete against cheaper ones
sie gehen wie warme Semmeln weg (inf)	they're selling like hot cakes
wie der Preis, so die Ware	you get what you pay for
sie verkaufen es mit Verlust	they're selling it at a loss
um den Marktanteil kämpfen	to fight for a market share
neue Kunden gewinnen	to win new customers
jdm 5 % Rabatt auf etw. geben	to give s.o. 5% discount on sth.
zum halben Preis verkaufen	to sell at half price
für etw. (+Acc) aufkommen	to pay for sth.

11.7 Aufschwung und Krise   Recovery and crisis

den Absatz steigern	to increase sales
bankrott/pleite sein	to be bankrupt
Bankrott/Pleite machen	to go bankrupt
rückläufig	declining
zahlungsunfähig	insolvent
das Geschäft wirft jetzt Gewinn ab/rentiert sich	the company is now showing a profit
rentabel/die Rentabilität	profitable/profitability
den Umsatz steigern	to raise turnover
das Geschäft blüht	business is booming
das Geschäft geht schlecht	business is slack
die Produktion drosseln	to cut back on production
einen Betrieb stilllegen	to close down a factory
schließen (ie-o-o) (itr)	to close down
in finanzielle Schwierigkeiten geraten (ä-ie-a)*	to get into financial difficulties
Arbeitskräfte entlassen (ä-ie-a)	to make workers redundant
€50 00 Schulden haben	to be €50 000 in debt
jdm. einen Kredit von €50 000 gewähren	to lend s.o. €50 000

11.8 Die Börse   Stock exchange

die Aktie (-n)	share, share certificate
der Aktienindex	shares index
der Aktionär (-e)	shareholder
die Baisse (-n)	bear market (falling)
der Börsenmakler (-)	stockbroker
an der Börse gehandelt	quoted on the stock exchange
der Börsensturz	collapse of share prices
erstklassig	blue-chip
der Ertrag (-̈e)	income, return, yield

die Fusion (-en)	merger
sein Geld in (+*Dat*) ... anlegen	to invest in ...
handeln mit	to deal in
die Hausse (-n)	bull market (rising)
die Investition (-en)	investment
der Kapitalanleger (-)	investor
die Marktkräfte (*pl*)	market forces
die Milliarde	a thousand million (US: billion)
der Spekulant (-en)	speculator
(an der Börse) spekulieren	to speculate (on the stock exchange)
die Spekulation mit Grundstücken	property speculation
die Übernahme (-n)	takeover
das Übernahmeangebot (-e)	takeover bid

an die Börse gehen	to float a company
der Markt erholt sich	the market is recovering
die Börse ist flau/lebhaft	trading is quiet/lively
diese Firma ist eine gute Kapitalanlage	this company is a good investment

11.9 Der internationale Handel International trade

die Abwertung	devaluation
das Außenhandelsdefizit	trade gap/deficit
die Einheitswährung	single currency
der Euro (-s)	the euro
die Europäische Währungsunion	European Monetary Union
die Handelsbilanz	balance of trade
die Handelsschranke (-n)	trade barrier
die Handelsziffern	trade figures
eine harte Währung	a stable currency
der Kurs (-e)	exchange rate, share price
der Protektionismus	protectionism
die Zahlungsbilanz	balance of payments
verdeckte Einkünfte	invisible earnings

wie steht der Kurs momentan?	what's the rate of exchange at the moment?
das Handelsvolumen hat sich rasch vergrößert	trade has increased rapidly in volume
die Erholung ist auf die Belebung des Auslandsgeschäfts zurückzuführen	the recovery is due to the upturn in foreign trade
der Dollar ist stark gefallen	the value of the dollar has dropped sharply
sein Anteil am gesamten Weltexport beträgt 5%	its share of world exports amounts to 5 %

seine Spitzenposition behaupten	to maintain its leading position
die BRD nimmt hinter den USA die zweite Stelle ein	Germany is in second place behind the USA
Großbritannien hat im Bereich Maschinenbau den Anschluss verpasst	Britain has missed the boat in the field of mechanical engineering
ihre Produkte sind qualitativ besser	their products are of better quality
sie sind auf britisches Know-how angewiesen	they rely on British know-how
eine schnell wachsende Wirtschaft	a tiger economy

11.10 Mein Einkommen   My income

der Abzug (⁼e)	deduction (from wages)
ohne Abzüge	before deductions (tax, etc.)
nach Abzug von Steuern	after tax
die Akkordarbeit	piecework
die Begüterten **die Einkommensstarken** }	the well-off
betriebliche Sozialleistungen	fringe benefits
das Einkommen	income
das Gehalt (⁼er)	salary
die Gehaltserhöhung (-en)	pay rise
das Jahreseinkommen	annual income
der Lohn (⁼e)	wage
das Prämiensystem	bonus scheme
die Steuer (-n)	tax
die Steuergruppe (-n)	tax bracket
die Steuervergünstigung (-en)	tax allowance
verdienen	to earn
die Vergünstigung (-en)	perk
der Zahltag	pay day
der gesetzliche Mindestlohn	statutory minimum wage
ihr Lohn liegt unter dem Existenzminimum	she's not earning a living wage
ein niedriges/mittleres Einkommen	a low/medium income
von der Hand in den Mund leben	to live from hand to mouth

11.11 Der Familienhaushalt   Family budget

ausgeben (i-a-e)	to spend (money)
die Ausgaben (pl)	outgoings
das ausgabefähige Einkommen	disposable income
bar bezahlen	to pay cash
das Bargeld	cash
besitzen (irreg)	to own

haftpflichtversichert sein*	to be insured third party
eine Hypothek über €200 000	€200 000 mortgage
die Kaufkraft	purchasing power
das Konto (*pl* Konten)	account
in einer Krankenkasse sein	to have health insurance
die Krankenversicherung (-en)	health insurance
die Kreditkarte (-n)	credit card
der Lebensstandard	standard of living
die Lebensversicherung (-en)	life insurance
die Miete (-n)	rent
etw. auf Raten kaufen	to buy sth. on hire purchase
eine Rechnung bezahlen	to settle a bill
schulden	to owe
verschwenden	to waste
die Vollkaskoversicherung (-en)	comprehensive insurance
der Wert (-e)	value
der Zins (-en)	interest

ich bin blank (*inf*)	I'm broke
der Anstieg der Lebenshaltungskosten	the rise in living costs
Einkommen und Ausgaben	income and expenditure
sie leben wie Gott in Frankreich	they live a life of luxury
sich nach der Decke strecken	to cut one's coat according to one's cloth
sich (*Dat*) den Gürtel enger schnallen	to tighten one's belt
über seine Verhältnisse leben	to live beyond one's means
seinen Verhältnissen entsprechend leben	to live within one's means
das kann ich mir nicht leisten	I can't afford that
in den roten Zahlen stecken	to be in the red
sie ist knapp bei Kasse	she's hard up
er hat Geldsorgen	he's got money problems
Geld allein macht nicht glücklich, aber es beruhigt	money alone doesn't make you happy, but it helps
das Geld aus dem Fenster werfen	to spend money like water

11.12 Die Banken — Banks

seine Bankgeschäfte telefonisch/ elektronisch erledigen	to do one's banking by phone/ electronically
das Darlehen (-)	loan
einzahlen	to pay in
die Geheimzahl eingeben	to tap in one's PIN
sich Geld leihen (ei-ie-ie)	to borrow money
Geld verleihen (ei-ie-ie)	to lend money

der Geldautomat (-en)	cash dispenser, cash machine
das Girokonto (-konten)	current account
das Konto ist überzogen	the account is overdrawn
der Kontoauszug (-̈e)	bank statement
die Kontoüberziehung	overdraft
die Kreditgrenze überschreiten (ei-i-i)	to go beyond one's credit limit
die Kreditkarte (-n)	credit card
das Online-banking	online banking
der Scheck (-s)	cheque
bar/mit Scheck bezahlen	to pay cash/by cheque
einen Scheck auf jdn. ausstellen	to make out a cheque to s.o.
eine Schuld abzahlen/tilgen	to pay off a debt
Soll und Haben	debit and credit
sparen für, auf (+Acc)	to save for
mein Sparkonto bringt 5 % Zinsen	my savings account pays 5% interest
das Telefonat (-e)	phone call
vertraulich	confidential
Geld auf sein Konto überweisen (ei-ie-ie) (insep)	to transfer money to one's account

---

Grundbegriffe

http://www.deutsche-wirtschaft.de *Informationsservice rund um die deutsche Wirtschaft*

http://www.diw.de *Deutsches Institut für Wirtschaftsforschung*

http://www.bundesfinanzministerium.de *Bundesministerium der Finanzen*

http://www.bundesbank.de/ *Deutsche Bundesbank*

http://www.zdh.de/ *Zentralverband des Deutschen Handwerks*

Die Wirtschaftspolitik

http://www.bmwi.de/ *Bundesministerium für Wirtschaft und Technologie*

http://www.bmwa.gv.at *Wirtschaft und Arbeit (Österreich)*

Der private Sektor/die Börse

http://www.vorsorgedurchblick.de *Informationen der Verbraucherzentralen*

http://deutsche-boerse.com/ *Gruppe Deutsche Börse*

www.boerse.de *die deutsche Börse*

Der internationale Handel

www.bfai.de *Bundesagentur für Außenwirtschaft*

http://www.eic.de/ *Euro Info Centre Deutschland*

12 Die Politik

der/die Abgeordnete (*adj. noun*)	Member of Parliament
abschaffen	to abolish
die Demokratie, demokratisch	democracy, democratic
die Demonstration (-en)	demonstration
die Europäische Union	the European Union
das Gesetz (-e)	law
an der Macht sein	to be in power
die Mehrheit	majority
die Meinung (-en)	opinion
die Opposition	opposition
die Politik (*no pl*)	politics, policy
der Politiker (-)	politician
die politische Partei (-en)	political party
protestieren	to protest
die Redefreiheit	freedom of speech
die Regierung (-en)	government
die Stimme (-n)	vote
die Wahlen (*pl*)	election
wählen/der Wähler (-)	to vote/voter
der Wahlkampf	election campaign

12.1 Die Staatsordnung — The system of government

der Außenminister (-)	Foreign Minister/Secretary
auf Bundesebene	at a national level
der Bundeskanzler (-)	Federal Chancellor
der Bundesrat	the Upper House (≈Lords)
der Bundestag (*Austria*: Nationalrat)	the Lower House (≈Commons)
der Finanzminister (-)	Finance Minister/Chancellor of the Exchequer
der Innenminister (-)	Home Secretary/Minister of the Interior
das Grundgesetz, die Verfassung	constitution
die Kabinettsumbildung	cabinet reshuffle
der Parteichef (-s)	party leader
eine Politik betreiben (ei-ie-ie)	to pursue a policy
der Sitz (-e) im Parlament; das Mandat	seat in parliament
der Sprecher (-)	spokesperson
das Staatsoberhaupt (¨er)	head of state
verfassungswidrig	unconstitutional

12.2 Die politischen Parteien   Political parties

Bündnis 90/die Grünen	the Greens
die CDU, die Konservativen	the Conservatives
die FDP, die Liberalen, liberal	the Liberals, liberal
die Parteienlandschaft	the political spectrum
die Linke	the Communists
sozialistisch, der Sozialismus	socialist, socialism
die SPD, die Sozialisten	the socialists, the Labour Party
der/die Links-(Rechts)radikale (-n)	left-(right-) wing extremist
der/die Gemäßigte (*adj. noun*)	moderate
kompromissbereit	prepared to compromise
konservativ/der Konservatismus	conservative/conservatism
mäßig	moderate
reaktionär/revolutionär	reactionary/revolutionary
totalitär	totalitarian

über den Parteien stehen	to stand above politics
dem rechten Flügel der Partei angehören	to be on the right of the party

12.3 Der Wahlkampf   The election campaign

A holt B langsam ein	A is catching up with B
an Boden gewinnen	to gain ground
die Meinungsumfrage (-n)	opinion poll
die Politikverdrossenheit	disenchantment with politics
skeptisch	sceptical
sich zur Wahl stellen	to stand for election
die Wählerschaft	electorate, constituents
das Wahlgeschenk (-e)	pre-election promise

einen Wahlkampf führen	to conduct an election campaign
seine Wahlversprechen einhalten (ä-ie-a)	to keep one's election promises
ihre Beliebtheit nimmt zu	she is gaining in popularity
Stimmen gewinnen/verlieren	to gain/lose support
jdm. vertrauen	to trust s.o.
seine Glaubwürdigkeit verlieren	to lose one's credibility
30 % der Befragten waren gegen ...	30% of those polled were against ...
Gott weiß was versprechen	to promise the earth
ein vom Grundgesetz garantiertes Recht (-e)	a right guaranteed by the constitution

12.4 Die Wahlen · The elections

für einen Kandidaten stimmen	to vote for a candidate
das Mehrheitswahlrecht	'first past the post', majority voting system
die Parlamentswahlen (pl)	general election
ein Referendum abhalten (ä-ie-a)	to hold a referendum
stimmberechtigt	entitled to vote
die Stimme (-n)	vote
der Stimmzettel (-)	ballot paper
zu den Urnen gehen (irreg)	to go to the polls
das Verhältniswahlrecht	proportional representation
der Wahlanteil	share of the vote (of a party)
das Wahlergebnis (-se)	election result
eine Wahl ankündigen	to call an election
eine hohe Wahlbeteiligung	a good turnout
die Wahlfälschung	vote-rigging
der Wahlkreis (-e)	constituency
das allgemeine Wahlrecht	right of every citizen to vote
das Wahlsystem	electoral system
gleiches Stimmrecht für alle	one man, one vote
ein überwältigender Sieg (-e)	a landslide victory
eine geringe/absolute Mehrheit	a small/absolute majority
ohne absolute Mehrheit	with no overall majority
eine vernichtende Wahlniederlage	a crushing electoral defeat
er wurde zum Präsidenten gewählt	he was elected president
sie wurde in den Bundestag gewählt	she was elected to parliament
eine Koalition bilden	to form a coalition government

12.5 Das Parlament · Parliament

der Ausschuss (-̈e)	committee
die Debatte (-n)	debate
ein Gesetz (-e) aufheben (e-o-o)	to repeal an act
ein Gesetz (-e) einbringen (irreg)	to introduce a bill
ein Gesetz (-e) verwerfen (i-a-o)	to throw out a bill
ein Gesetz (-e) verabschieden	to pass a bill
kuzfristige Maßnahmen (pl)	short-term measures
langfristige Maßnahmen (pl)	long-term measures
rechtskräftig werden (irreg)	to become law
eine Regierung bilden	to form a government
die Sitzung (-en)	sitting, meeting
zurücktreten (i-a-e)*	to resign

eine stürmische Debatte über (+Acc) ...	a stormy debate on ...
über einen Antrag (⁻e) abstimmen	to vote on a proposal
auf der Tagesordnung stehen	to be on the agenda
unter Leitung des Bundeskanzlers	under the leadership of the Federal Chancellor
vom Bundeskanzler ernannt	appointed by the Federal Chancellor

12.6 Das politische Leben   Political life

aufrührerisch	inflammatory
fordern	to demand
die Kehrtwendung	about-turn
kontrovers, umstritten	controversial
kritisieren	to criticise
nachgeben (i-a-e)	to give way
eine Rede halten (ä-ie-a)	to make a speech
die Unterschriftensammlung (-en)	petition
auf zunehmenden Widerstand stoßen (ö-ie-o)*	to meet with increasing resistance
behaupten, dass zwei mal zwei fünf ist	to argue that black is white
es birgt die Gefahr, dass ...	it involves the danger that ...
eine Demonstration veranstalten	to hold a demonstration
eine Diskussion auslösen	to provoke discussion
eine durchgreifende Reform fordern	to demand a complete reform
Fragen von weitreichender Bedeutung	questions of far-reaching importance
gegen energisch vorgehen ...	to take a tough line on ...
den Kopf in den Sand stecken	to bury one's head in the sand
radikale Maßnahmen ergreifen	to take radical measures
die Reform zu einem Eckpfeiler seiner Politik machen	to make reform a cornerstone of one's policy
die Sache schleifen lassen	to drag one's feet
Schwung verlieren (ie-o-o)	to lose momentum
er sieht den Wald vor lauter Bäumen nicht	he can't see the wood for the trees
die straffe Führung	strong leadership
eine Tat verurteilen	to condemn an action
wegen der öffentlichen Kritik	due to public criticism
sich weigern nachzugeben	to refuse to back down
zu Auseinandersetzungen führen	to lead to disagreements
die künftige Politik muss darauf abzielen, ...	future policy must aim to ...
die Krise ist überwunden worden	the crisis has been resolved
in einer andauernden Krise stecken	to be in a continuing crisis

12.7 Die Kommunalverwaltung Local government

die Behörden (*pl*)	the authorities
der (Ober-)Bürgermeister (-)	(lord) mayor
die Gemeinde (-n)	local authority, local community
der Gemeinderat, Stadtrat (⁻e)	town council/councillor
die Gewerbesteuer (-n)	local business tax
die Gemeindeverwaltung	local authority
auf Landesebene	at state/*Land* level
der Landtag	state/*Land* government
die Polizei ist Landessache	the police is the responsibility of the *Land*

12.8 Die Europäische Union The European Union

die Europäische Kommission	European Commission
das Europäische Parlament	European Parliament
der Europäische Binnenmarkt	European internal market
die Europäische Zentralbank	European Central Bank
die Entscheidungsbefugnisse (*pl*)	decision-making powers
der Föderalismus	federalism
die föderative Struktur	federal structure
die Gemeinsame Agrarpolitik	Common Agricultural Policy
der Mitgliedsstaat (-en)	member state
die Währungsunion	single currency
die Wirtschaftsintegration	economic integration
die Zusammenarbeit der Mitgliedsstaaten	the cooperation of member states
die Abhängigkeit der Landwirtschaft von Subventionen abbauen	to reduce the dependency of agriculture on subsidies
die Abschaffung der Grenzen	the removal of borders
an der Spitze aller Handelsmächte stehen	to be the leading economic power
der Anteil am Welthandel	share of world trade
den Ausbau der Wirtschafts- beziehungen fördern	to promote the extension of economic links
die Ausführung der Gemeinschaftsbeschlüsse durch die Mitgliedsstaaten	the implementation of Community decisions by member states
am Entscheidungsprozess beteiligt sein	to be involved in the decision-making process

der freie Verkehr von Personen, Waren, Dienstleistungen und Kapital	the free movement of people, goods, services and capital
es führt zu Überschüssen (*pl*)	it leads to overproduction
Handelshindernisse abbauen	to remove barriers to trade
eine politisch handlungsfähige Union	a Community capable of taking (joint) political action
steuerliche Schranken abbauen	to remove tax barriers
den Wohlstand der Bürger vermehren	to improve the prosperity of its citizens
eine Reform erzwingen/fordern	to force/demand a reform

12.9 Die deutsche Wiedervereinigung

German reunification

die Berliner Mauer	the Berlin Wall
der Demokratisierungsprozess	process of democratisation
die ehemalige DDR ⎫ die neuen Bundesländer ⎭	what used to be the GDR
der Eiserne Vorhang	the Iron Curtain
die Geheimpolizei	secret police
inhaftieren	to arrest
der Kalte Krieg	the Cold War
konkurrenzfähig	competitive
die Kosten der Einheit	the cost of unity
die Ostalgie	nostalgia for the supposed advantages of the former GDR
der Spitzel (-); jdn. bespitzeln	informer; to inform on
stürzen	to overthrow
Truppen (*pl*) abziehen	to withdraw troops
der Umbruch	upheaval, radical change
unterdrücken	to suppress, oppress
die Überwachung	surveillance
der Wiederaufbau	reconstruction
der Übergang zu einer Marktwirtschaft	the transition to a market economy
eine Demonstration gewaltsam zerschlagen	to break up a demonstration by violent means
den Regierungssitz von Bonn nach Berlin verlegen	to move the capital from Bonn to Berlin

Die Staatsordnung
http://www.oesterreich.com/ *Informationen über Österreich*
http://www.bundestag.de/ *Deutscher Bundestag*
www.bundesrat.de *Deutscher Bundesrat*
http://www.parlament.ch/ *das Schweizer Parlament*
http://www.parlament.gv.at/ *Österreichisches Parlament*
http://www.austria.gv.at/ *Bundeskanzleramt Österreich*
http://www.firstlink.li/ *Fürstentum Liechtenstein*

Die Parteien/der Wahlkampf
http://www.gruene.de *Bündnis 90/Die Grünen*
http://www.cdu.de/ *Christlich Demokratische Union*
www.spd.de *Sozialdemokratische Partei Deutschlands*
http://www.fdp.de/ *Freie Demokratische Partei Deutschlands*
http://www.sozialisten.de *die Linkspartei*
http://www.w-asg.de/ *WASG die Wahlalternative*

Die Wahlen
http://www.wahlrecht.de/ *Wahlen, Wahlrecht und Wahlsysteme*
http://www.election.de/ *Wahlen in Deutschland*
www.wahl-o-mat.de *Bundeszentrale für politische Bildung*

Die Europäische Union
http://www.europa.eu.int/ *the European Union online*
http://www.europarl.de/ *Europäisches Parlament*
www.eu-kommission.de *die Vertretung der Europäischen*
Kommission in Deutschland

Die Deutsche Wiedervereinigung
http://www.wiedervereinigung.de/ *Informationen zur Wiedervereinigung*
http://www.dhm.de/lemo/html/DieDeutscheEinheit/ *die deutsche Einheit*
http://www.chronik-der-wende.de/ *Chronik der Wende 7. Oktober 1989*
http://www.die-wende.de/ *Informationen zur Wende*

Verschiedenes
http://www.bpb.de/ *Bundeszentrale für politische Bildung*
http://www.politik.de/ *das Portal für die politische Seite im Internet*
http://www.politikerscreen.de/ *Informationsdienst für Politik*

13 Internationale Beziehungen

die Abrüstung	disarmament
die Armee, das Heer	army
das Attentat (-e)	terrorist attack
die Dritte Welt	the Third World
der Feind (-e), der Gegner (-)	enemy
friedlich/der Frieden	peaceful/peace
die Großmächte (pl)	super powers
internationale Beziehungen (pl)	international relations
kämpfen/der Kampf (¨e)	to fight/fight
der Konflikt (-e)	conflict
einen Konflikt schlichten	to resolve a conflict
der Krieg (-e)	war
das Militär	the military, armed forces
die Niederlage (-n)	defeat
das Opfer (-)	victim
siegen (itr), der Sieger (-)	to win, the victor
der Soldat (-en)	soldier
der Terrorist (-en), der Terrorismus	terrorist, terrorism
überfallen (ä-ie-a)	to attack
die Vereinten Nationen, die UNO	United Nations (Organisation)
verteidigen	to defend
die Waffe (-n)	weapon
der Widerstand	resistance
zerstören	to destroy

13.1 Die Außenpolitik   Foreign policy

ein Abkommen schließen (ie-o-o)	to sign a treaty
der Alliierte (adj. noun) ⎫ der Allianzpartner (-) ⎭	ally
die Atommächte	atomic powers
der Atomwaffensperrvertrag	nuclear non-proliferation treaty
diplomatische Beziehungen abbrechen (i-a-o)	to break off diplomatic relations
die Botschaft/der Botschafter	embassy/ambassador
der Diplomat, die Diplomatie	diplomat, diplomacy
diplomatisch vorgehen (irreg)	to use diplomacy
über etw. Einigung erzielen	to reach agreement on sth.
die Entspannung	easing of tensions
die Friedenstruppen (pl)	peace-keeping force

die Machtbalance	balance of power
die Macht ergreifen (ei-i-i)	to seize power
die Menschenrechte (*pl*)	human rights
die Menschenrechtsverletzung (-en)	abuse of human rights
die NATO-Mitgliedschaft	NATO membership
scheitern*	to break down, fail
der Truppenabbau	troop reductions
Truppen abziehen (ie-o-o)	to withdraw troops
Truppen stationieren/einsetzen	to station/deploy troops
etw. vereinbaren	to agree on sth.
verhandeln/die Verhandlung (-en)	to negotiate/negotiation
jdm. etwas vorwerfen (i-a-o)	to accuse s.o. of sth.

(über jdn.) die Oberhand gewinnen	to gain the upper hand (over s.o.)
am Scheideweg stehen	to have reached a crossroads
einen Vertrag billigen	to ratify a treaty
in einem Streit vermitteln	to act as conciliator
die Verhandlungen scheitern	the talks break down
Friedensverhandlungen führen	to hold peace talks
Maßnahmen zur Sicherung des Friedens	peace-keeping measures
die Beschwichtigung (durch Zugeständnisse)	appeasement (by making concessions)
einen bedeutsamen Beitrag zu … leisten	to make a significant contribution to …
wirtschaftliche Sanktionen (*pl*) aufstellen gegen …	to set up economic sanctions against …
ein Ölembargo verhängen	to impose an oil embargo

13.2 Der Krieg   War

die Abrüstung/die Aufrüstung	disarmament/acquisition of armaments
angreifen (ei-i-i)/der Angriff (-e)	to attack/the attack
eine Atomstreitmacht sein	to possess a nuclear capability
die Atomwaffe (-n)	atomic weapon
besetzen	to occupy (land)
die Besatzungsarmee (-n)	occupying army
besiegen (*tr*)	to defeat
beschießen (ie-o-o)	to shell, shoot at
der Bürgerkrieg (-e)	civil war
einmarschieren in (+*Acc*)	to invade
die ethnische Säuberung	ethnic cleansing
erobern	to conquer
erschießen (ie-o-o)	to shoot (and kill) s.o.
der Flüchtling (-e)	refugee
die Friedensbewegung	peace movement
gegeneinander kämpfen	to fight against one another

grausam/der Gräuel (-)	cruel, terrible/atrocity
die Invasion	invasion
die Massenvernichtungswaffen (pl)	weapons of mass destruction
der Pazifismus	pacifism
die Schlacht (-en)	battle
einen Sieg erringen (i-a-u)	to win a victory
überleben (insep)	to survive
überrennen (insep) (mixed verb)	to overrun
umbringen/töten	to kill
umstellen (insep)	to surround
sich (+Dat) unterwerfen	to submit to
verletzen	to wound
der/die Vertriebene (adj. noun)	exile

sie kämpfen um ihre Freiheit	they're fighting for their freedom
den Krieg vermeiden	to avoid war
jdm. den Krieg erklären	to declare war on s.o.
idm Krieg stehen	to be at war
einen Krieg gewinnen (i-a-o)	to win a war
die militärische Intervention	military intervention
für den Krieg rüsten	to arm for war
der Krieg zu Wasser, zu Lande und in der Luft	the war at sea, on land and in the air
jdm. ein Ultimatum stellen	to deliver an ultimatum to s.o.
ums Leben kommen* (o-a-o)	to lose one's life
verwüsten	to lay waste to
schnelles Handeln war erforderlich	swift action was needed
der Waffenstillstand	ceasefire
Widerstand leisten	to offer resistance

13.3 Die Streitkräfte   The armed forces

abschaffen	to abolish
die Abschreckung	deterrent
die allgemeine Wehrpflicht	national (military) service, conscription
das Atominferno	nuclear holocaust
der Berufssoldat (-en)	professional soldier
biologische/chemische Waffen	biological/chemical weapons
die Bundeswehr	(German) armed forces
der Geheimdienst	secret service
das Kampfflugzeug (-e)	warplane
konventionelle Waffen (pl)	conventional weapons
der Kriegsdienstverweigerer (-)	conscientious objector
das Kriegsschiff (-e)	warship
seinem Land dienen	to serve one's country
die Langstreckenwaffe (-n)	long-range weapon

die Luftwaffe/die Marine	air force/navy
der Marschflugkörper (-)	cruise missile
marschieren	to march
der Offizier (-e)	officer
der Panzer (-)	tank
die Rakete (-n)	missile
der Spion (-e)/die Spionage	spy/espionage
der Spionagesatellit (-en)	spy satellite
der Stützpunkt (-e)	base (military)
die Truppen (*pl*)	troops
das Verteidigungsministerium	Ministry of Defence
der Waffenhandel	the arms trade
die Wehrpflicht	military service, conscription
der Zivildienst	community service (rather than military service)

einem Kommando gehorchen	**to obey a command**
Einsparungen (*pl*) im Verteidigungshaushalt	**savings in the defence budget**
der Gemeinschaft dienen	**to serve the community**
seinen Militärdienst ableisten	**to do one's military service**

13.4 Der Terrorismus   Terrorism

einen Anschlag verüben	to carry out an attack
sich zu einem Anschlag bekennen	to admit carrying out an attack
der Attentatsversuch (-e)	assassination attempt
ausliefern nach (+*Dat*)	to extradite to
einer Bombe zum Opfer fallen (ä-ie-a)	to be the victim of a bomb
eine Bombe zünden	to set off a bomb
der Bombenanschlag (⁻e)	bomb attack
der Bombenalarm	bomb alert
der Entführer (-)	hijacker
ermorden	to murder
der Fanatiker (-)	fanatic
ein Flugzeug entführen	to hijack a plane
foltern	to torture
der Gegenschlag (⁻e)	reprisal
die Geisel (-n)	hostage
jdn. als Geisel nehmen	to take s.o. hostage
hetzen gegen (+*Acc*)	to stir up hatred against
hinrichten	to execute
kaltblütig	cold-blooded
der Selbstmordanschlag (⁻e)	suicide bomb attack
der Selbstmordattentäter (-)	suicide bomber
die Sicherheitsdienste (*pl*)	security services
töten	to kill

großen Schaden anrichten	to cause great damage
der islamische Fundamentalist (-en)	Islamic fundamentalist
der Kampf gegen den Terrorismus	fight against terrorism
politisch motiviert	politically motivated
wahllos angreifen (ei-i-i)	to strike indiscriminately
ein Verbrechen an der Menschheit	crime against humanity
Forderungen nachgeben	to give in to demands
einen festen Standpunkt vertreten	to take a firm stand
überall Abscheu auslösen/ hervorrufen	to provoke widespread disgust
unannehmbare Forderungen stellen	to make impossible demands
ein ziviles Ziel angreifen (ei-i-i)	to attack a civilian target

13.5 Die Dritte Welt   The Third World

abgemagert	emaciated
der/die AIDS-Kranke (*adj. noun*)	AIDS victim
der Analphabetismus	illiteracy
die Armut bekämpfen	to fight poverty
die Auslandsverschuldung	foreign debt
die Bevölkerungsexplosion	population explosion
die Dürre (-n)	drought
das Elend lindern	to alleviate misery
die Entwicklungshilfe	development aid
die Entwicklungsländer (*pl*)	developing countries
das Erdbeben (-)	earthquake
der Erdrutsch (-e)	landslide
Familienplanung betreiben	to practise family planning
fördern	to support, to aid
die Geburtenkontrolle	birth control
der Geburtenzuwachs	increase in the birth rate
die Hilfsorganisation (-en)	aid organisation
leiden (ei-i-i) unter (+*Dat*)	to suffer (from)
die Hungersnot/verhungern	famine/to die of starvation
die karitative Organisation (-en)	charity
die Korruption	corruption
das Krisengebiet (-e)	crisis zone
die Naturkatastrophe (-n)	natural disaster
niedrige Lebenserwartungen	low life expectancy
die Säuglingssterblichkeit	infant mortality
die Schuldenkrise	debt crisis
die Seuche (-n)	epidemic
die Spende (-n)/spenden	donation (to charity)/to donate
die Überbevölkerung	overpopulation
die Überschwemmungen (*pl*)	floods
unterentwickelt	underdeveloped
die Unterernährung	malnutrition

die Waise (-n), das Waisenkind (-er)	orphan
zur Waise werden	to be orphaned
der Waldbrand (-̈e)	forest fire
das Wirtschaftswachstum	economic growth

eine Sammlung für karitative Zwecke	a collection for charity
eine 10 Meter hohe Flutwelle	a tidal wave 10m high
die ungleiche Verteilung	unequal distribution
der krasse Unterschied zwischen Arm und Reich	the huge gulf between rich and poor
zur Selbsthilfe anleiten	to help people to help themselves
unter der Armutsgrenze leben	to live below the poverty line

Die Außenpolitik

http://www.dgap.org/   *Deutsche Gesellschaft für Auswärtige Politik e.V.*
http://www.auswaertiges-amt.de/   *Auswärtiges Amt*
http://www.deutsche-aussenpolitik.de/   *Deutsche Außenpolitik*
http://www.bnd.bund.de/   *Bundesnachrichtendienst*

Der Krieg/der Terrorismus

http://www.sef-bonn.org/   *Stiftung Entwicklung und Frieden*
http://www.bundeswehr.de   *Deutsche Bundeswehr*
http://www.friedensrat.ch/   *Schweizerische Friedenspolitik*
http://www.zivildienst.de/   *Bundesamt für den Zivildienst*
http://www.terrorismus.de/   *Informations-Portal Terrorismus*

Die Dritte Welt

http://www.bmz.de   *Bundesministerium für wirtschaftliche Zusammenarbeit und Entwicklung*
http://www.entwicklungshilfe.de/   *Internationale Elementar-Hilfe e.V.*
http://www.epo.de/   *Entwicklungspolitik online*
http://www.welthungerhilfe.de/   *Welthungerhilfe*

14 Soziale Fragen

Die Einwanderung | Immigration

um Asyl bitten (i-a-e)	to seek asylum
der Asylant/der Asylbewerber	asylum seeker
jdn. diskriminieren	to discriminate against s.o.
der Einwanderer (-)	immigrant
der Flüchtling (-e)	refugee
der Hass/hassen	hatred/to hate
hetzen gegen	to stir up hatred against
integrieren/die Integration	to absorb, integrate/integration
die Menschenrechte	human rights
das Misstrauen, misstrauen (+Dat)	mistrust, to mistrust
die Lebensart (-en)	way of life
die multikulturelle Gesellschaft	multicultural society
der Rassismus/der Rassist	racism/racist

14.1 Flüchtlinge und Asylanten | Refugees and asylum seekers

das Asylrecht	the right to asylum
Asyl erhalten	to be granted asylum
die Arbeitsgenehmigung (-en)	work permit
die Aufenthaltserlaubnis (-e)	residence permit
das Aufenthaltsrecht	the right to residence
der ausländische Arbeitnehmer (-)	foreign worker
der Bürger (-)	citizen
die ethnische Minderheit	ethnic minority
fliehen vor (+Dat) (ie-o-o)	to flee from
die Gleichberechtigung	equal rights
das Herkunftsland (-er)	country of origin
das Notaufnahmelager (-)	reception centre, transit camp
repatriieren	to repatriate
die Ungleichheit	inequality
die Unterdrückung	oppression
verfolgen	to persecute
der Vertriebene (adj. noun)	refugee, exile
der Wirtschaftsflüchtling (-e)	economic migrant

der Anteil der Ausländer an der Bevölkerung liegt bei n %	there is an immigrant population of n%
wegen ihrer politischen Überzeugung	because of their political views
Flüchtlinge aufnehmen	to admit/absorb refugees
einen Asylantrag billigen/ablehnen	to approve/turn down an application for asylum
über eine Arbeitserlaubnis verfügen	to have a work permit
er hat das Recht auf Einbürgerung in die BRD	he has the right to German citizenship
die doppelte Staatsbürgerschaft	dual nationality
Eingliederungsgeld erhalten	to receive financial aid (to assist integration)

14.2 Die Probleme für das Gastland
Problems for the host country

der Aufnahmestopp	ban on immigration
das Einwanderungsland das Aufnahmeland (-̈er)	host country
die Freizügigkeit	freedom of movement
das Ghetto	ghetto
der Zuzug (-̈e)	influx
die Wirtschaft kann ausländische Arbeitskräfte nicht entbehren	the economy cannot do without foreign workers
Ehegatten folgen ihren Partnern	spouses join their partners
sie holen ihre Familien nach	they bring their families over
die soziale Integration	social integration
eine arrangierte Ehe	an arranged marriage
sie wohnen geballt in bestimmten Regionen	they live predominantly in certain areas
Asylgesetze (pl) verschärfen	to tighten up the law on the granting of asylum
den Zuzug von Flüchtlingen möglichst gering halten	to keep the influx of immigrants as low as possible
finanzielle Anreize (pl) zur Rückkehr in die Heimat die Rückkehrhilfe	financial incentives to return home

14.3 Die Probleme der Einwanderer
Problems for the immigrants

sich abkapseln	to cut/shut oneself off
sich einleben	to settle down
die Hautfarbe	skin colour

die Herkunft	background, origin
kulturelle Unterschiede (*pl*)	cultural differences
schwarzarbeiten	to work illegally, without a permit
sich auf Deutsch mündlich verständigen können	to be able to make oneself understood in German
die kulturelle Identität wahren	to maintain one's cultural identity
Ausländer der zweiten Generation	second generation immigrants
vom sozialen Aufstieg ausgeschlossen	excluded from social advancement
in ihre Heimat zurückkehren*	to return home
andere Länder, andere Sitten	other countries, other customs

14.4 Der Rassismus   Racism

der Antisemitismus	anti-Semitism
die Ausländerfeindlichkeit ⎫ der Fremdenhass ⎬	hatred of foreigners
der Brandanschlag (⁻e)	arson attack
die Eskalation	escalation
der Neonazismus	neo-Nazism
die Rassendiskriminierung	racial discrimination
der Rassenkrawall (-e)	race riot
die Rassenunruhen (*pl*)	racial disturbances
Rassenvorurteile (*pl*) haben	to be racially prejudiced
schikanieren	to harass, bully
terrorisieren	to terrorise
tolerant/die Toleranz	tolerant/tolerance
die Überfremdung	swamping with foreigners
das Wiederaufleben	resurgence
wieder auftauchen	to resurface
zusammenschlagen	to beat up
die Feindseligkeit	hostility
leiden unter (+*Dat*) (ei-i-i)	to suffer from
den Groll anfachen	to fuel resentment
Ängste ausnutzen	to play on fears
der kulturelle Konflikt	cultural clash
die kulturelle Vielfalt	cultural diversity
eine rassistische Äußerung	a racist comment
auf Rassismus zurückzuführen	racially motivated
auf beiden Seiten	on both sides
sie werden wie Bürger zweiter Klasse behandelt	they are treated like second-class citizens

Die Religion — Religion

jdn. anbeten	to worship s.o.
der Christ (-en), christlich	Christian
das Gewissen	conscience
glauben an +Acc/der Glaube	to believe in/faith, belief
die Glaubensfreiheit	religious freedom
gläubig	religious (=having belief)
Gott verehren	to worship God
der Gottesdienst	service (in church, etc.)
Gutes tun	to do good
in die Kirche gehen	to go to church
die Meditation, meditieren	meditation, to meditate
menschlich, göttlich	human, divine
moralisch, die Moral	moral, morality
die Theologie	theology
die Unmoral, unmoralisch	immorality, immoral

14.5 Glaube im Alltag — Faith in practice

der Aberglaube, abergläubisch	superstition, superstitious
der Agnostizismus, der Agnostiker	agnosticism, agnostic
der Atheismus, der Atheist	atheism, atheist
die Auferstehung	the Resurrection
bekehren, der Bekehrte (adj. noun)	to convert s.o., convert
beten	to pray
beweisen (ei-ie-ie)	to prove
die Bibel	the Bible
das Christentum	Christianity
die Diakonie	social/welfare work of churches
Jesus Christus	Jesus Christ
evangelisch	Protestant
das Evangelium	the Gospel, the gospels
der Fundamentalismus	fundamentalism
die Gewissensfrage	a question of conscience
der Gläubige (adj. noun)	believer
Gut und Böse	good and evil
heilig	holy, sacred
der Islam, islamisch	Islam, Islamic
der Judaismus, jüdisch	Judaism, Jewish
der Jude (-n)/die Jüdin (-nen)	Jew (masc/fem)
katholisch	Catholic
der Koran	Koran

das Kreuz	cross
die Lehre (-n)	doctrine
der Materialismus	materialism
das Mitleid	pity, sympathy
die Moschee (-n)	mosque
das (moslemische) Kopftuch	the muslim headscarf
der Muslim (-e)	muslim
der Papst	the Pope
der Pfarrer (-)	priest, vicar
predigen	to preach
weltlich	secular
die Seele (-n)	soul
der Selbstmordanschlag (¨e)	suicide bomb attack
der Selbstmordattentäter (-)	suicide bomber
die Sünde (-n)	sin, wrongdoing
die Synagoge (-n)	synagogue
der Teufel	the Devil
vergeben (i-a-e)	to forgive
die Versöhnung	reconciliation
die Weltanschauung (-en)	philosophy of life, world view
der Zeitgeist	spirit of the times, *zeitgeist*

in die Kirche gehen (*irreg*)	to go to church
ein reines/schlechtes Gewissen haben wegen (+*Gen*)	to have a clear/guilty conscience about
die Zehn Gebote	the Ten Commandments
das Vaterunser	the Lord's Prayer
du sollst nicht töten	thou shalt not kill
Glaube, Liebe, Hoffnung	faith, hope and charity
liebe deinen Nächsten	love your neighbour
das Leben nach dem Tod	life after death
in den Himmel kommen	to go to heaven
in die Hölle kommen	to go to hell
die Vergangenheitsbewältigung	coming to terms with the guilt of the past (in Germany)

der Atheismus führte zu den schlimmsten Kriegen des 20. Jahrhunderts	atheism led to the worst wars of the 20th century

Die soziale Ausgrenzung   Social exclusion

arbeitslos	unemployed
arm/die Armut	poor/poverty
benachteiligt	disadvantaged, deprived
der Drogenhändler	drug dealer

der Drogensüchtige (*adj. noun*)	drug addict
elend, erbärmlich	squalid
das Elendsviertel (-)	sink estate, slum
die Gewalt	violence
die Graffiti	graffiti
die Kriminalität	crime
schlecht bezahlt	poorly paid
sich langweilen	to be bored
der Vandalismus	vandalism

14.6 Die Armut   Poverty

die Arbeitslosigkeit	unemployment
die Armutsfalle	poverty trap
besetzen/der Hausbesetzer (-)	to occupy, squat/squatter
betteln	to beg
der Bettler (-)	beggar
die Gang (-s), die Bande (-n)	gang
heimatlos, obdachlos	homeless
die Obdachlosigkeit	homelessness
die Jugendkriminalität	juvenile delinquency
die Kleinkriminalität	petty crime
die Sachbeschädigung	damage to property
der Schulversager (-)	failure at school (person)
der Sozialabbau	cuts in social services
die Sozialhilfe	income support
der Sozialhilfeempfänger (-)	person receiving income support
die Sozialmobilität	social mobility
die Sozialwohnung (-en)	council flat
der Straßenraub (*no pl*)	mugging
der Teufelskreis	vicious circle
unterqualifiziert/unqualifiziert	underqualified/unskilled
die Unterschicht	the underclass
sich verbessern	to better onseself
das Wohngeld	housing benefit
die Wohnverhältnisse (*pl*) } die Wohnbedingungen (*pl*) }	living conditions

die Einelternfamilie	**single-parent family**
Angst haben vor (+*Dat*)	**to fear**
an Straßenecken herumlungern	**to hang around on street corners**
ohne festen Wohnsitz	**of no fixed abode**
im Freien übernachten	**to sleep rough**
von der Hand in den Mund leben	**to live from hand to mouth**
von zu Hause weglaufen	**to run away from home**

die **Betuchten** und die **Habenichtse**	the haves and the have-nots
unterhalb der Armutsgrenze leben	to live below the poverty line
niedrige Löhne	low wages
sich über Wasser halten (ä-ie-a)	to make ends meet
die **Null-Bock-Generation**	completely apathetic generation
die **mangelnde Werteorientierung**	lack of any sense of moral values
von Arbeitslosigkeit stark betroffen	badly affected by unemployment

Die Einwanderung
http://www.migration-online.de/ *Migration online*
http://www.bamf.de *Migration und Flüchtlinge*
http://www.integrationsbeauftragte.de/ *Migration, Flüchtlinge und
Integration*
http://www.zuwanderung.de/ *Zuwanderungsrecht in Deutschland*
http://www.einbuergerung.de/ *das neue Staatsbürgerschaftsrecht*
http://www.auslaender-statistik.de/ *Ausländer-Statistik*

Die Probleme für die Einwanderer
http://www.prointegration.org/ *Integration für Zuwanderer*
http://www.isoplan.de/aid/ *AiD – Integration in Deutschland*

Flüchtlinge und Asylanten
http://www.asyl.at/ *Asylkoordination Österreich*
http://www.asyl.de/ *Migration in Deutschland und Europa*

Der Rassismus
http://www.dir-info.de/ *Rassismusforschung*
http://www.lpb.bwue.de/zauberw/rechtsra.htm *Rechtsradikalismus*
http://www.idgr.de/ *Informationsdienst gegen Rechtsradikalismus*
http://www.antisemitismus.net/ *Antisemitismus*
http://www.verfassungsschutz.de/ *Bundesamt für Verfassungsschutz*

Religion
http://www.ekd.de/ *Evangelische Kirche in Deutschland*
http://www.katholische-kirche.de *Katholische Kirche in
Deutschland*
http://www.juden.de *Informationen über das Judentum*
http://www.judentum.net *siehe oben*
http://islam.de *Informationen über den Islam*

Armut
http://www.armut.ch/ *Jugendarmut*
http://www.mehr-freiheit.de/faq/armut.html *Wer ist arm?*
http://www.schader-stiftung.de/wohn_wandel/805.php *Arbeitslosigkeit
und Ausgrenzung im Wohnquartier*
http://www.eundc.de *Regiestelle E&C – Entwicklung und Chancen
junger Menschen in sozialen Brennpunkten*

15 Die Rechtsordnung

Note that there are many differences between the German legal system and those of Britain or the USA; take great care when looking for equivalents in, for instance, courts or procedures.

der Drogenhändler	drug dealer
der Dieb (-e)	thief
jdn. festnehmen (i-a-o)	to arrest s.o.
das Gesetz (-e)	law, statute
(un)gerecht	(un-)just
ins Gefängnis kommen	to go to prison
gewalttätig/die Gewalttätigkeit	violent/violence
die Kriminalität	crime
legal, illegal	legal, illegal
das Opfer (-)	victim
der Personalausweis (-e)	ID card
die Polizei	police
der Polizist (-en)	police officer
das Polizeirevier	police station
stehlen (ie-a-o)	to steal
der Straftäter (-)	criminal
der Kriminelle (*adj. noun*)	
der Überfall (⁻e)	mugging (incident)
der Vandalismus	vandalism
verbieten (ie-o-o)	to ban
ein Verbrechen begehen (*irreg*)	to commit a (serious) crime
die Waffe (-n), die Schusswaffe (-n)	weapon, fire-arm

15.1 Die Rechtsordnung   Legal system

das Arbeitsrecht	labour law
die Gerechtigkeit	justice
das Gericht (-e)/vor Gericht	court/in court
gesetzlich	by law
der Jurist (-en)	lawyer
etw. kriminalisieren	to make sth. a criminal offence
legalisieren	to legalise
die Menschenrechte (*pl*)	human rights
der Prozess (-e)	trial
der Rechtsstaat	the rule of law
das Recht	justice, legal system, right
der Rechtsanwalt (⁻e)	lawyer, barrister

der Richter (-)	judge
schützen vor (+*Dat*)	to protect from
der Staatsanwalt (⁻e)/die Staatsanwältin (-nen)	public prosecutor
das Völkerrecht	international law
das Gesetz verletzen	to break the law
einen Rechtsanspruch auf etw. haben	to be within one's rights to do sth.
das Recht beanspruchen, etw. zu machen	to claim the right to do sth.
der Bürger wird dadurch in seinen Rechten verletzt	this violates basic civil rights
die Verordnung (-en)	by-law, local regulation
etw. für rechtmäßig erklären	to make sth. legal
in Kraft treten (i-a-e)*	to come into force
das Bundesverfassungsgericht	constitutional court
die Todesstrafe abschaffen	to abolish the death penalty

15.2 Das Privatrecht — Civil law

die Beleidigung ⎫ die Verleumdung ⎭	slander, libel
jdn. auf etw. (+*Acc*) verklagen	to sue s.o. over sth.
den Rechtsweg einschlagen	to take legal proceedings
eine Sache vor Gericht bringen	to go to court over sth.
die Scheidung einreichen	to sue for divorce
sie bekam €n Schadensersatz zugesprochen	she was awarded €n damages

15.3 Das öffentliche Recht — Criminal law

ahnden	to punish
das Bagatelldelikt (-e)	petty crime (individual act)
die Kleinkriminalität	petty crime (activities)
die Bestechung	bribery
der Betrug/der Betrüger	fraud/crook
der Datenschutz	data protection
der Diebstahl (⁻e)	theft
der Einbrecher (-)	burglar
der Einbruch (⁻e)	burglary
ergaunern (*tr*)	to get sth. by dishonest means
die Erpressung	blackmail
die Geldwäsche	money-laundering
der Ladendiebstahl	shoplifting
missbrauchen	to misuse
der Mittäter (-)	accomplice

mutmaßlich	suspected
der Pädophile (*adj. noun*)	paedophile
eine Parkkralle anlegen	to wheel-clamp
die Steuerhinterziehung	tax evasion
die Straftat (-en)	criminal offence
der Taschendieb (-e)	pickpocket
die Trunkenheit am Steuer	drunken driving
die Unterschlagung	embezzlement
der Verbrecher (-)	criminal
das Verkehrsdelikt (-e)	traffic offence
kriminell leben	to lead a life of crime
kriminell werden (*irreg*)	to become a criminal
die organisierte Kriminalität	organised crime
ein kleineres Vergehen	a minor offence
gegen das Gesetz verstoßen* (ö-ie-o)	to break the law
der Vorbestrafte (*adj. noun*)	person with a criminal record
einen Bankraub verüben	to commit a bank robbery
mit Diebesgut handeln	to receive stolen goods
die Sachbeschädigung	damage to property
mutwillig beschädigt	damaged by vandals
in Untersuchungshaft nehmen	to take into custody
personenbezogene Daten	personal data
in die Hände von Unbefugten gelangen*	to fall into the wrong hands
schwarzarbeiten	to work without a permit, to moonlight
schwarzfahren*	to travel without a ticket/ drive without a licence
die Zahl der Verbrechen nimmt zu	crime is on the increase

15.4 Die Gewalt   Violence

der Bandenkrieg (-e)	gang warfare
bewaffnet	armed
einschüchtern	to intimidate
entführen	to kidnap
ermorden	to murder, assassinate
jdn. erschießen (ie-o-o)	to shoot s.o. dead
gewaltsam	by force
grundlos, ohne Anlass	unprovoked
kaltblütig	in cold blood
die Kindesmisshandlung	child abuse
die schwere Körperverletzung	grievous bodily harm
der Mord (-e) (an jdm.)	murder (of s.o.)
der Mörder (-)	murderer
auf jdn. schießen (ie-o-o)	to shoot at s.o.

die Schießerei (-en)	shoot-out, gun battle
die Schlägerei (-en)	(fist) fight
der Schuss (-̈e)	shot
die Stecherei (-en)	stabbing
der Straßenraub	mugging (category of crime)
jdn. überfallen (*insep*) (ä-ie-a)	to attack, mug
die Vergewaltigung	rape
jdn. zusammenschlagen (ä-u-a)	to beat s.o. up

ein bewaffneter Raubüberfall	armed robbery
in Notwehr handeln	to act in self-defence
die Gewalt als Mittel der	violence as a means of dealing
Konfliktlösung	with conflict
ein Lösegeld verlangen	to demand a ransom
er schoss sie in den Arm	he shot her in the arm

15.5 Die öffentliche Ordnung   Public order

die Bereitschaftspolizei	riot police
die Gang (-s), die Bande (-n)	gang
friedlich	peaceful
der Fußballrowdy	football hooligan
gesetzestreu	law-abiding
die Jugendkriminalität	juvenile delinquency
der jugendliche Straftäter	young offender
der Krawall (-e)	riot
die Ordnungskräfte (*pl*)	law and order
das Rowdytum	hooliganism
unsozial	anti-social

eine Demonstration veranstalten	to hold a demonstration
außer Kontrolle geraten (ä-ie-a)*	to get out of hand
etw. in Brand stecken	to set fire to sth.
das Recht selbst in die Hand	to take the law into one's own
nehmen	hands
das Rowdytum bekämpfen	to combat thuggery

15.6 Die Polizei   Police

die Aufklärungsquote	detection rate
aufspüren	to track down
die DNS-Tests (*pl*)	DNA fingerprinting, tests
entkommen* (o-a-o)	to escape
die Fahndung	search
die Festnahme (-n)	arrest
jdn. festnehmen (i-a-o)	to arrest s.o.
die Fingerabdrücke (*pl*)	finger prints
der Kriminalbeamte (*adj. noun*)	detective

die Kriminalpolizei	CID
die Kriminaltechnik	forensic science
die Null-Toleranz-Strategie	zero-tolerance strategy
das Phantombild (-er)	identikit picture
die Schutzausrüstung	riot gear
die Spur (-en)	clue
der Streifenwagen (-)	patrol car
das Tränengas	tear gas
das Überfallkommando	riot police
untersuchen	to investigate, search
die Verbrechensbekämpfung	the fight against crime
die Verbrechensrate	crime rate
die Verbrechensverhütung	crime prevention
verhaften	to arrest
jdn. vernehmen (i-a-o), verhören	to question s.o.
die Polizei fährt in diesem Viertel Streife	the police patrols this area
eine Razzia (pl Razzien) machen	to raid, make a swoop on
gegen jdn. ermitteln	to investigate s.o.
in einem Fall ermitteln	to investigate a case
ein Verbrechen aufklären	to solve a crime
einen Verbrecher fangen (ä-i-a)	to catch a criminal
einen Dieb fassen	to catch a thief
jdn. auf frischer Tat ertappen	to catch s.o. red-handed
jdn. beim Einbrechen stellen/ erwischen	to catch s.o. breaking in
jm. Handschellen anlegen	to handcuff s.o.
jdn. auf das Polizeirevier bringen	to take s.o. to the police station
er bleibt in Untersuchungshaft	he's been remanded in custody
man hat sie auf Kaution freigelassen	she's out on bail
in die Tüte blasen (ä-ie-a)	to be breathalysed
bei (+Dat) hart durchgreifen	to clamp down on

15.7 Vor Gericht — In court

der Angeklagte (*adj. noun*)	defendant, accused (person)
jdn. (wegen +*Gen*) anklagen	to charge s.o. (with)
die Anklage	charge, accusation
die Anklagevertretung	counsel for the prosecution
der (Augen)Zeuge (-n)	(eye-)witness
für/gegen jdn. aussagen	to give evidence for/against s.o.
die Aussage (-n)	statement
Berufung einlegen	to appeal
beweisen (ei-ie-ie)	to prove
das Beweismaterial	evidence
jdn. freisprechen (i-a-o)	to acquit s.o.
der Gefangene	prisoner

ins Gefängnis kommen (o-a-o)	to go to prison
hart	severe
die Jugendstrafanstalt (-en)	detention centre for young offenders
jdn. kriminalisieren	to criminalise s.o.
leugnen	to deny
milde, die Milde	lenient, leniency
die Schöffen (*pl*)	jury
sich (nicht) schuldig bekennen	to plead (not) guilty
jdn. (nicht) schuldig sprechen (i-a-o)	to find s.o. (not) guilty
jdn. strafrechtlich verfolgen	to prosecute s.o.
überfüllt	overcrowded
das Urteil verkünden	to pass sentence
die Verteidigung	counsel for the defence
widerlegen	to disprove
die Zelle (-n)	cell

ihr Fall kam vor Gericht	her case came before the court
vor Gericht erscheinen* (ei-ie-ie)	to appear in court
unter Mordanklage stehen (*irreg*)	to be on a murder charge
er wurde des Mordes angeklagt	he was charged with murder
auf der Anklagebank sitzen (*irreg*)	to be in the dock
jdn. ins Kreuzverhör nehmen (i-a-o)	to interrogate s.o.
jdn. als Zeugen vorladen (ä-u-a)	to call a witness
der genetische Fingerabdruck ist als Beweismittel zugelassen	genetic fingerprinting is permitted as evidence
etw. in Frage stellen	to call sth. into question
einen Meineid leisten	to commit perjury
das Verbrechen gestehen (*irreg*)	to confess to a crime
aus Mangel an Beweisen	due to insufficient evidence
einen Täter überführen	to convict a criminal
die Strafe soll dem Verbrechen angemessen sein	the punishment should fit the crime
eine harte Linie verfolgen	to take a hard line
härtere Strafen sind kein Heilmittel	harsher penalties are not the answer
jdn. zu einer Geldstrafe verurteilen	to fine s.o.
sie muss €100 Strafe bezahlen	she's been fined €100
er wurde mit einer Geldstrafe belegt	he was punished with a fine
ihm wurde der Führerschein für 1 Jahr entzogen	he lost his driving licence for a year
jdn. ins Gefängnis schicken	to send s.o. to prison
die lebenslängliche Freiheitsstrafe	life sentence
er wurde zu 6 Monaten Haft verurteilt	he was sentenced to 6 months imprisonment
man gab ihm ein Jahr Bewährung	they put him on probation for a year

Verbrechen lohnen sich nicht   crime doesn't pay
die Wiedereingliederung   reintegration (into society)

Die Rechtsordnung
http://www.bmj.bund.de   *Bundesministerium der Justiz*
http://www.institut-fuer-menschenrechte.de   *Menschenrechte*
http://www.buergerliches-gesetzbuch.info/   *Bürgerliches Gesetzbuch*
http://www.rechtsstaat.de   *Rechtsstaat, Politik, Gesetze*
http://www.rechtsstaat-austria.com/   *Rechtsstaat Österreich*
http://www.fahndungsgruppe.de   *Alkohol und Drogen im Straßenverkehr*
http://www.gesetze-im-internet.de/   *Gesetze im Internet*

Die öffentliche Ordnung
www.dji.de   *Deutsches Jugendinstitut*
http://www.gewaltpraevention-elternarbeit.de/   *Psychologische Aspekte von Jugendgewalt und Jugendkriminalität*
http://www.weisser-ring.de   *Kriminalitätsopfer und ihre Familien*

Die Polizei
www.bka.de   *Bundeskriminalamt*
http://www.polizei.de/   *die offizielle Seite der deutschen Polizei*
http://www.die-kriminalpolizei.de/   *die Kriminalpolizei*

Vor Gericht
http://www.bundesverfassungsgericht.de/   *die Verfassung*
http://www.der-jugendrichter.de/   *der Jugendrichter*

Verschiedenes
http://www.planet-tegel.de/   *Internetseite von Gefangenen*

16 Die Umwelt

das Abwasser	sewage
die Atomenergie/die Kernenergie	atomic energy
aussterben (i-a-o)*	to become extinct
der Boden	soil
dreckig, schmutzig	dirty
die Energie/die Energiequelle (-n)	energy/energy source
Energie sparen	to save energy
das Erdöl	oil
erneuerbar	renewable
die Erwärmung der Erdatmosphäre	global warming
die Folge (-n)	consequence
gefährden, gefährlich	to endanger, dangerous
die Gewässer	lakes and rivers
die Industrie	industry
die Katastrophe (-n)	catastrophe
die Konsumgesellschaft	consumer society
die Landwirtschaft	agriculture
die Luft	air
der Müll	rubbish, waste
recyceln (hat ... recycelt)	to recycle
schädlich	damaging
schützen (vor +Dat)	to protect (from)
die See (-n), das Meer (-e)	sea
die Umwelt	environment
umweltfreundlich	environmentally friendly
der Umweltschutz	environmental protection
der Verbraucher (-)	consumer
verschmutzen, belasten	to pollute
wegwerfen (i-a-o)	to throw away

16.1 Die Probleme   The problems

die Ausbeutung	exploitation
die Gefährdung (+Gen)	danger (to)
das Gift (-e), vergiften	poison, to poison
konsumieren, verbrauchen	to consume, use
künstlich	artificial
rücksichtslos	thoughtless
schaden (+Dat)	to damage
die Übervölkerung	overpopulation

die Umwelt	environment
umweltfeindlich	damaging to the environment
die Verschmutzung	pollution
vernichten, zerstören	to destroy
verschmutzen, belasten } verpesten, verseuchen }	to pollute
verschwenden	to waste
vergiften	to poison
der Umweltsünder (-)	polluter

im Laufe unseres Lebens	in the course of our lives
viele Opfer fordern	to claim many victims
umweltfreundliche Produkte (pl)	environmentally friendly products
voll/frei von Schadstoffen	full/free of harmful substances
der Umweltschutz ist ein wichtiges politisches Thema geworden	the protection of the environment has become an important political issue
vom Menschen ausgelöste Faktoren verursacht	from man-made causes

16.2 Die Folgen The consequences

die Auswirkung (-en)	effect
bedrohen	to threaten
die Flutwelle (-n)	tidal wave
gesundheitsgefährdend	damaging to health
das Gewitter (-)	storm
die Immission	effect on neighbouring property of pollution (gases, noise, etc.)
katastrophal	catastrophic
die Überschwemmung (-en)	flood
die Verwüstung	devastation
warnen vor etw. (+Dat)	to warn of sth.
zurückgreifen auf (+Acc) (ei-i-i)	to fall back on

das Abschmelzen der Polkappen	melting of ice-caps
der Anstieg des Meeresspiegels	rise in sea-level
die Klimaveränderungen (pl)	climate change
der Treibhauseffekt	greenhouse effect
die Überflutung der Küstenstreifen	flooding of coastal regions
vom Aussterben bedrohte Tierarten	species threatened with extinction
es hat beängstigende Ausmaße erreicht	it has reached a worrying level
bis zum Beginn des nächsten Jahrhunderts	by the beginning of the next century
die Bedrohung der Menschen	threat to humanity

in den Naturhaushalt eingreifen (ei-i-i)	to upset the balance of nature
man sagt voraus, dass ...	it is forecast that ...
die Folgen (pl) voraussagen	to predict the consequences
die Folgen sind kaum absehbar	it's hard to say what the consequences will be
um kommender Generationen willen	for the sake of future generations
das wird uns teuer zu stehen kommen	that will cost us dear
es wird Millionen in Elend stürzen	it will plunge millions into poverty
was bleibt dann übrig?	what will be left?

16.3 Die Gegenmaßnahmen   Counter-measures

sich anstrengen	to increase one's efforts
mindern	to reduce
retten	to save
mit etw. (+Dat) sparsam umgehen	to use sth. economically
das Umweltbewusstsein	environmental awareness
das Umweltbundesamt	Department of the Environment (government)
die Umwelterziehung	environmental education
die Umweltpolitik	environmental policy
die Umweltsteuer, Ökosteuer (-n)	environmental tax
der Umweltverstoß (⸚e)	action damaging to the environment
sich zu etw. (+Dat) verpflichten	to commit oneself to sth.
das Verständnis verstärken	to increase one's understanding
vorsorglich	as a precaution
sparsam (im Verbrauch)	economical (in consumption)
wir sind von ... (+Dat) abhängig	we depend on ...
es gibt kein Zurück	there's no going back
Gegenmaßnahmen (pl) einleiten	to introduce counter-measures
grenzüberschreitende Regelungen	cross-border agreements
das Gesetz verschärfen	to tighten up the law
... hätte zur Folge, dass ...	... would have the effect that ...
wir müssen schon entstandene Schäden (pl) beseitigen	we must repair damage which has already been done
die Schadstoffbelastung mindern	to reduce damage by pollutants
die Schäden (pl) eindämmen	to contain the damage
den Umweltschutz in die Praxis umsetzen	to put environmental conservation into practice
auf die Umweltverschmutzung aufmerksam machen	to raise awareness of environmental pollution
eine Wende in der öffentlichen Einstellung zum Umweltschutz	a change in the public's attitude to environmental conservation
wenn zu ihrer Rettung nichts unternommen wird	if nothing is done to save them

ökonomische und ökologische Interessen abwägen	to balance economic and ecological interests
... gilt als unverzichtbar	... is thought to be indispensable
um das Überleben der Menschheit zu sichern	in order to ensure the survival of humanity
... stellt ein Problem für die Industrie dar	... represents a problem for industry
die langfristigen Auswirkungen bewerten	to assess the long-term effects

16.4 Die Luft   Air

das Auspuffrohr (-e)	exhaust pipe (of vehicle)
die Brennstoffzelle (-n)	fuel cell
bleifrei tanken	to use unleaded petrol
die Emission (-en)	emission (of gas, etc.)
es entsteht durch ...	it results from ...
freisetzen	to release
die Geschwindigkeitsbegrenzung (-en)	speed limit
das Gift (-e)	poison
der Katalysator	catalytic convertor
das Kohlendioxid	carbon dioxide, CO_2
der Kohlenstoff	carbon
der Krebsauslöser/krebserregend	cancer-causing agent/carcinogenic (adj.)
das Kühlmittel (-)	coolant
die Ozonschicht	ozone layer
das Ozonloch	hole in the ozone layer
quellen (i-o-o)* aus	to pour from
der saure Regen	acid rain
der Ruß	soot
der Sauerstoff	oxygen
das Schwefeldioxid	sulphur dioxide, SO_2
der Stickstoff	nitrogen
die Steuervorteile (pl)	tax incentives
das Waldsterben	destruction of forests by acid rain
der Wasserstoff	hydrogen
giftige Abgase (pl) abgeben	to give off poisonous waste gases
in die Atmosphäre blasen	to pump into the atmosphere
Autofahrer am Rasen hindern	to make drivers slow down
Autos müssen reduzierten Abgasnormen genügen	cars have to meet stricter exhaust controls
ehemals dicht bewaldete Flächen (pl)	what were once thickly forested areas
der geringe Benzinverbrauch	low fuel consumption
die Korrosionsschäden (pl) an Gebäuden	corrosion damage to buildings

ultraviolette (UV-) Strahlen (*pl*)	ultraviolet (UV) rays
ein vermehrtes Auftreten von Hautkrebs	an increased incidence of skin cancer
die Verkehrsberuhigung	traffic-calming

16.5 Das Wasser — Water

industrielle Abwässer (*pl*)	industrial effluent
die Kläranlage (-n)	sewage treatment plant
einen Ölteppich beseitigen	to clean up an oil slick
der Stausee (-n)	reservoir
das Trinkwasser	drinking water
die Überfischung	over-fishing
die Wasserversorgung	water supply
die Wasservorräte (*pl*)	water reserves

die Anrainerstaaten (*pl*) der Nordsee	countries bordering on the North Sea
die Aufnahmekapazität des Meeres für Schadstoffe	ability of the sea to absorb pollutants
Chemikalien in Gewässer ablassen	to release chemicals into rivers, lakes
in das Grundwasser sickern	to seep into the ground water

16.6 Der Boden — The soil

die Bodenerosion	soil erosion
die Dürre	drought
die Entwaldung	deforestation
die Entwässerung	drainage
das Land/den Wald roden	to clear land/forest
das Naturschutzgebiet (-e)	nature reserve
der Regenwald (⁼er)	rain forest
der Rohstoffabbau	mining of raw materials
die Rückstände (*pl*)	residues

die Ansammlung von Pestiziden (*pl*) im Boden	the build-up of pesticides in the soil
Schadstoffe gelangen* über die Nahrungskette in den Körper	pollutants reach the body by way of the food chain
die Bio-Lebensmittel (*pl*)	organic food
die ökologische Landwirtschaft	organic agriculture
den Regenwald vernichten	to destroy the rain forest
mit Urwald bedeckt	covered with virgin forest
ein empfindliches Öko-System	a delicate ecosystem
gefährdete Tier- und Pflanzenarten	threatened animal and plant species
hohe Nitratgehalte (*pl*)	high concentrations of nitrates

die intensive Landwirtschaft	intensive farming
in Gebieten mit intensiver Landwirtschaft	in areas with intensive agriculture
die steigende Agrargüter-Erzeugung	rising agricultural production
künstliche Düngemittel (pl)	artificial fertilisers

16.7 Der Müll — Rubbish

die Abfallentsorgung	waste disposal
die Abfalltrennung	separation of rubbish into plastics, paper, etc.
die Alu-Dose (-n)	aluminium can
der Autoschrott	scrap cars
die Einwegflasche (-n)	non-returnable bottle
fertigen, herstellen	to manufacture
der Hausmüll	household rubbish, waste
die Kartonage (-n)	cardboard packaging
der Kunststoffcontainer (-)	plastic container
die Mehrwegflasche (-n)	returnable bottle
die Müllabfuhr	refuse collection
die Mülldeponie (-n)	rubbish dump
der Mülleimer (-)	dustbin
die Müllverbrennungsanlage	refuse incinerator plant
die Pfandflasche (-n)	returnable bottle
die Plastiktüte (-n)	plastic bag
recyceln, wiederverwerten	to recycle
recyclebar, wiederverwertbar	recyclable
das Recycling	recycling
der Schrott	scrap metal
die Sondermüllsammelstelle (-n)	collection point for old paint, oil, etc.
der Sperrmüll	bulky items of refuse
die Verklappung	dumping of industrial waste at sea
die Verpackung (-en)	packaging
wegschmeißen/wegwerfen	to throw away

Abfälle auf die Straße werfen	**to drop litter in the street**
die Abfallvermeidung	**ways of reducing amount of waste**
aus Altpapier	**made from recycled paper**
biologisch abbaubar	**biodegradable**
leere Flaschen zum Altglascontainer bringen	**to take empty bottles to the glass recycling skip**
50 Cent Pfand auf der Flasche	**50 cent deposit on the bottle**
der Mangel an Rohstoffen (pl)	**the shortage of raw materials**
den Müll getrennt sammeln	**to collect types of rubbish separately**
es kommt alles in den Mülleimer	**it all goes into the dustbin**

die wilde Müllkippe (-n)	illegal rubbish dump
Rohstoffe (pl) wiedergewinnen	to reclaim raw materials
zu neuen Produkten verarbeiten	to turn into new products

16.8 Fossile Brennstoffe — Fossil fuels

das Benzin	petrol, gas (USA)
der Brennstoff	fuel (e.g. for heating)
der Diesel(kraftstoff)	diesel (fuel)
der Energiebedarf	energy requirements
der Energieverbrauch	energy consumption
die Erdölförderländer (pl)	oil-producing countries
die Erdölförderung	oil production
die Erdölraffinerie (-n)	oil refinery
erschöpft werden	to run out
die Kohle	coal
der Kraftstoff	fuel (for engine)
das Gas	gas
die Ölvorräte	oil reserves
die Pipeline (-s), die Rohrleitung (-en)	pipeline
das Rohöl	crude oil
der Preis fiel auf $n je Barrel	the price fell to $n a barrel

16.9 Die Atomenergie — Atomic energy

der Brennstoff	fuel
die Brennstäbe (pl)	fuel rods
der Dampf	steam
das Kernkraftwerk (KKW)	nuclear power station
der Kernreaktor, der Atomreaktor	nuclear reactor
die Kernschmelze	meltdown
außer Kontrolle geraten (ä-ie-a)	to get out of control
die Strahlung	radiation

zum Antrieb von Turbinen einsetzen	to use to drive turbines
ein Atomkraftwerk stilllegen	to close down a nuclear power station
ein Atomkraftwerk in Betrieb nehmen (i-a-o)	to commission a nuclear power station
der Ausstieg aus der Atomenergie	the move away from atomic energy
die Endlagerung radioaktiver Abfälle	the storage of radioactive waste
der Gau (größter anzunehmender Unfall)	MCA (maximum credible accident)
sollten wir das Risiko eingehen?	should we take the risk?
die Wiederaufbereitungsanlage (WAA)	nuclear reprocessing plant

16.10 Erneuerbare Energiequellen — Renewable energy sources

energiesparend	energy-saving
die geothermische Energie	geothermal energy
die Gezeitenenergie	tidal power
die Sonnenenergie	solar energy
die Solarzellen (pl)	solar cells
die Wasserkraft	hydroelectric power
die Wellenenergie	wave power
die Windenergie	wind power
die Windfarm (-en)	wind farm

alternative Energiequellen entwickeln	to develop alternative energy sources
der Beitrag zum globalen Energieverbrauch	the contribution to total energy consumption
das ist hier nicht zu verwirklichen	this could not be put into effect here
sie werden schon kommerziell betrieben	they are already in commercial use
sie können nicht kontinuierlich Energie liefern	they cannot supply energy constantly
ihr Einsatz wird eingeschränkt durch (+Acc) ...	their use is limited by ...
der Ausbau dieser Anlagen wird vorgesehen	further building of these plants is planned
den Verbrauch auf das Nötigste einschränken	to limit consumption to the minimum

16.11 Konservierung zu Hause — Conservation at home

die Doppelfenster (pl)	double glazing
große/geringe Energiegewinne (pl)	large/small energy savings
isolieren/die Isolierung	to insulate/insulation
die dreifache Verglasung	triple glazing
heizen	to heat
lüften	to ventilate
schonen	to conserve
auf etw. (+Acc) verzichten	to do without sth.

die Regelanlage einstellen	to adjust the time/temperature unit
dadurch könnte man bis zu 20 % Energie sparen	by this method energy savings of up to 20% could be made
ein besserer Ausnutzungsgrad	more efficient use

Die Gegenmaßnahmen
http://www.bund.net/   *Bund für Umwelt und Naturschutz Deutschland*
http://www.umweltschutz.co.at/   *Magazine zum Umweltschutz*
http://www.europarc-deutschland.de   *Europarc Deutschland*
http://www.bfn.de/   *Bundesamt für Naturschutz*
http://www.nabu.de/   *NABU – Naturschutzbund Deutschland e.V.*
www.duh.de   *Deutsche Umwelthilfe e.V.*
http://www.klimasuchtschutz.de/   *Klimaschutzkampagne*

Luft/Wasser/Boden
http://www.dehst.de/   *Deutsche Emissionshandelsstelle*
http://www.gewaesserschutz-ev.de/   *Gewässerschutz*
http://www.bodenwelten.de/   *Informationsportal zum Thema Boden*

Der Müll
http://www.gruener-punkt.de/   *der Grüne Punkt – Duales System*
http://www.bvse.de   *das Recycling-Netz*

Die Energie
http://www.kernenergie.de/   *Informationen über Atomkraft*
http://www.energie-fakten.de/   *Informationen zu Energie und Umwelt*
http://www.bsi-solar.de/   *Bundesverband Solarindustrie e.V.*
http://www.wind-energie.de/   *Bundesverband Windenergie e.V.*
http://www.erneuerbare-energien.de/   *erneuerbare Energien*
http://www.strom.de   *Verband der Elektrizitätswirtschaft*
http://www.erdgasinfo.de/   *Informationen über Erdgas*
http://www.mwv.de/   *Mineralölwirtschaftsverband e.V.*

Verschiedenes
http://www.umweltbundesamt.de/   *Umweltbundesamt*
http://www.bmu.de/   *Umwelt, Naturschutz und Reaktorsicherheit*
http://www.umwelt-schweiz.ch   *Bundesamt für Umwelt (Schweiz)*
http://www.lebensministerium.at/   *Bundesministerium für Land- und
          Forstwirtschaft, Umwelt und Wasserwirtschaft (Österreich)*
http://www.geowissenschaften.de/   *das Magazin für Geo- und
                              Naturwissenschaften*

17 Technik und Forschung

der Computer (-)	computer
das Computerspiel (-e)	computer game
einloggen, ausloggen	to log on, to log off
(ein)tippen	to type (in)
downloaden, herunterladen	to download
entwickeln	to develop
die Folge (-n)	consequence
die Forschung/forschen über (+Acc)	research/to research into
das Handy (-s)	mobile phone
das Internet	the internet
im Internet surfen	to surf the internet
innovativ	innovative
eine Krankheit ausmerzen	to eradicate a disease
jdm. mailen	to e-mail someone
die Raumfahrt	space travel
rechtfertigen	to justify
die SMS, jdn. simsen	text message, to text someone
ein uralter Traum	an ancient dream
die Textverarbeitung	word processing
einen Versuch machen	to carry out an experiment
die Webseite (-n)	web page

Many computer terms are identical in both English and German, with the gender given by the ending or the related German word (e.g. -er = masc; das Notebook (=das Buch))

Masc: Computer, Cursor, Cyberspace, Hacker, Laptop, Monitor, PC, Provider, Scanner, Server, Virus
Fem: CD-ROM, Diskette, E-Mail, Homepage, Hotline, Hardware, Software
Neut: Format, Icon, Keyboard, Modem, Notebook, Programm, Terminal, Update

17.1 Die Hardware — Hardware

der Anschluss, der Port	port
die Akkulaufzeit	battery life
der Bildschirm (-e)	screen
der CD-Brenner	CD writer
der Drucker	printer
die Festplatte (-n)	hard disk
handlich	pocket-sized

der Flachbildschirm	flat screen
der MP3-Player	MP3 player
der drahtlose Internetzugang	wireless internet access
das Ladegerät (-e)	(mains) charger
die Maus (¨e)	mouse
die Patrone (-n)	cartridge
der Speicher	memory
die Tastatur/das Keyboard	keyboard
tragbar	portable

mein Computer stürzt die ganze Zeit ab	my computer keeps crashing
Songs auf die Festplatte laden (ä-u-a)	to download songs onto the hard drive
auf eine CD brennen	to burn onto a CD
auf einen MP3-Spieler überspielen	to download onto an MP3 player

17.2 Die Software — Software

abspeichern	to save
abstürzen*	to crash
anklicken	to click on
anwenderfreundlich	user-friendly
das Anwenderprogramm	application program
aufrufen	to call up
aufrüsten/upgraden	to upgrade
ausdrucken	to print out
bearbeiten	to edit
der Befehl (-e)	command
booten/neu starten	to (re)boot
die Datei (-en)	file
die Datenbank (-en)	database
Datenkopien erstellen	to make a back-up
das Datenschutzgesetz	data protection law
einblenden, einfügen	to insert
eingeben, eintippen	to enter (data), to key in, type in
das Fenster	window
die Graphik	graphics
das Hauptmenü	main menu
installieren	to install
die Klangkulisse	sound effects
kleben	to paste
die künstliche Intelligenz	artificial intelligence
löschen	to delete
das Netzwerk	network
das Passwort, Kennwort (¨er)	password
der Programmfehler (-)	bug

scannen/einscannen	to scan in
die Shift-/Escape-Taste	shift/escape key
die Schriftart (-en)	font
sichern	to back up (work)
die Spacetaste/Leertaste	space key
die Textverarbeitung	word-processing
das Verzeichnis (-se)	directory
wiederfinden (i-a-u)	to retrieve
die Wissensexplosion	the information explosion

Computer dringen in fast alle Lebensbereiche ein	computers affect almost every aspect of our lives
Computerviren vernichten den Datenbestand	computer viruses destroy stored data
die Papiermenge reduzieren	to reduce the volume of paper
Viren/einen Virus auffinden	to detect viruses/a virus

17.3 Das Internet — The internet

der Anschluss per Modem	link via a modem
das Breitband	broad band
die Datenübertragung	data transmission
die elektronischen Medien	the electronic media
sich erkundigen nach (+*Dat*)	to find out about
gewaltverherrlichend	violent (in content)
der Info-Stress	information overload
der Internet-Nutzer (-)	internet user
der Internetzugang	internet access
die Kindersicherung	child protection
seine E-Mails lesen (ie-a-e)	to look at one's e-mails
online sein*	to be online
das Online-Banking	online banking
die Online-Dienste	online services
(zu)spammen	to spam
die Suchmaschine (-n)	search engine
auf Tastendruck	at the push of a button
uploaden/hochladen	to upload
mit Werbung bombardieren	to spam (advertising)

die Informationsgesellschaft	information technology-based society
anstößige Inhalte aussortieren	to filter out offensive material
mit pornographischen Beiträgen konfrontiert werden	to be confronted with pornographic material

17.4 Die Kommunikation   Communications

die Akte (-n)	file
der Aktenschrank (-̈e)	filing cabinet
der Anhang (-̈e)	attachment (i.e. file)
jdn. anrufen/mit jdm. telefonieren	to phone s.o.
nach Köln telefonieren	to phone Cologne
archivieren	to store
die Dezentralisierung	decentralisation
die Digitalkamera (-s)	digital camera
die Digitaltechnik	digital technology
ein Dokument per Telefax schicken ⎫ ein Dokument faxen ⎭	to fax a document
die elektronische Post	electronic mail
das Faxgerät (-e)	fax machine
das Ferngespräch (-e)	long-distance call
die Freisprechanlage (-n)	hands free kit (for mobile)
die Gesprächsgebühren (*pl*)	call charges
das Glasfaserkabel	optical fibre cable
der Klingelton (-̈e)	ring tone
das Ortsgespräch (-e)	local call
das schnurlose Telefon	cordless telephone
jdm. etw. ausrichten lassen (ä-ie-a)	to leave s.o. a message
die Telefongebühr (-en)	call charge
die SMS, jdn. simsen	text message, to text someone
der Strichkode	bar code
das Telefax	fax
die Telearbeit	teleworking, working outside the office
das Telefonat (-e)	phone call
das Telefonverzeichnis (-se)	phone directory
die Voicemail	voicemail

über die Telefonleitung übermitteln	to transmit by telephone line
die Büroarbeit rationalisieren	to make office work more efficient
fast alle Haushalte verfügen **über (+Acc) ...**	almost all homes have ...
von Routinetätigkeiten entlasten	to free from routine chores
man ist immer erreichbar	people can always reach you
neue Dienste anbieten	to offer new services

17.5 Die Industrie   Industry

beschleunigen	to speed up
ersetzen	to replace
die Fertigungstechnik	production technology
der Technologiepark (-s)	science park

die Auswirkungen (*pl*) auf die Arbeitsplätze	effect on jobs
menschliche Arbeitskraft durch Technik ersetzen	to replace human labour by technology
Arbeitsplätze wegrationalisieren	to destroy jobs
die Fertigungsstraße (-n)	production line
am Fließband arbeiten	to work on the production line
Zeit- und Kostenaufwand verringern	to cut costs and time
der Ausbau wachstumsstarker Technologien	the development of fast-growing technologies
es unterliegt einem schnellen Wandel	it's undergoing rapid change

17.6 Die Forschung — Research

durch Ausprobieren	by trial and error
bahnbrechend	pioneering
Forschung und Entwicklung (FuE)	research and development (R&D)
der Fortschritt (-e)	progress
die Innovation (-en)	innovation
das Laboratorium (-rien) } das Labor (-s)	laboratory
die Lebensqualität	quality of life
eine Methode perfektionieren	to perfect a technique
ein Problem lösen	to solve a problem
das Reagenzglas (⁻er)	test-tube
die Technik	technology
verbessern	to improve
zurückliegen (ie-a-e)	to lag behind

Bahnbrechendes leisten	to pioneer new developments
ein Problem bewältigen	to overcome a problem
Wirklichkeit werden*	to become reality
die Forschung fördern	to support research
eine neue Phase einleiten	to mark the start of a new phase
die Blaupause für ...	the blueprint for ...
Abhilfe schaffen	to take remedial action
mit der herkömmlichen Technik	with present-day technology
bis zum Jahr(e) 2020 wird man ...	by the year 2020 they'll ...
muss man alles machen, was machbar ist?	do we have to do everything just because it's possible?
die meisten Menschen wollen nicht zum Sklaven der modernen Technik werden	most people don't want to become slaves of modern technology
ein ressortübergreifendes Programm	a cross-disciplinary programme

neueste Forschungsergebnisse (*pl*)	latest research findings
Pionierarbeit für etw. (+*Acc*) leisten	to pioneer sth.
an der Spitze stehen	to be in the lead
führend auf diesem Gebiet ist ...	the leader in this field is ...
jdm. um Lichtjahre voraus sein	to be light years ahead of s.o.

17.7 Die Weltraumforschung   Space research

die Atmosphäre	atmosphere
außerirdische Lebewesen	extraterrestrial life form
die Erde	Earth
neue Erkenntnisse gewinnen (i-a-o)	to gain new knowledge
das Hydrogen, der Wasserstoff	hydrogen
der Kommunikationssatellit (-en)	communications satellite
das Lichtjahr (-e)	light year
die Milchstraße	the Milky Way
eine Million, eine Milliarde	million, billion
Millionen und Abermillionen	millions and millions
der Mond (-e)	moon
das Oxygen, der Sauerstoff	oxygen
der Planet (-en)	planet
die Rakete (-n)	rocket
das Raumfahrtprogramm	space programme
der Raumflug (⁻e)	space flight
der Raumkörper (-)	(unmanned) space capsule
der Raumtransporter (-)	space shuttle
die Raumsonde (-n)	space probe
die Raumstation (-en)	space station
der Satellit (-en)	satellite
der Spionagesatellit (-en)	spy satellite
der Stern (-e)	star
das Sternsystem (-e)	galaxy
in die Umlaufbahn schießen	to send into orbit
der Weltraum, das All	space
in den Weltraum schießen (ie-o-o)	to launch into space
das Weltraumteleskop	space telescope
die Weltraumwaffe (-n)	space weapon

17.8 Die medizinische Forschung   Medical research

der Behandlungserfolg (-e)	successful treatment
der Empfänger (-)	recipient
genehmigen	to permit
das Heilmittel	cure (e.g. drug)
das Heilverfahren	cure (=treatment)
herstellen	to produce, manufacture
der Herzschrittmacher	pace-maker

die Kosmetika (*pl*)	cosmetics
Neben- und Nachwirkungen	side- and after-effects
die Pharmaindustrie	pharmaceutical industry
jdn. quälen	to inflict suffering on s.o.
Schmerzen lindern	to relieve pain
ein schmerzstillendes Mittel	painkiller
die Seuchenbekämpfung	battle against epidemics
der Spender (-)	donor
der Superbazillus	superbug
verpflanzen	to transplant
die Vogelgrippe	avian flu
einen Versuch machen	to carry out an experiment
das Versuchskaninchen (-)	guinea-pig (for research)

als Versuchskaninchen verwenden	to use as a guinea-pig
ein Heilmittel für Krebs entwickeln	to develop a cure for cancer
Versuche an Tieren einstellen	to halt experiments on animals
die Risiken (*pl*) für den Patienten vermindern	to lower the risks to the patient
sich einer Organverpflanzung unterziehen (ie-o-o; *insep*)	to undergo an organ transplant
ein geschädigtes Organ ersetzen	to replace a damaged organ
das Organ abstoßen (ö-ie-o)	to reject the organ
neue medizinische Verfahren	new medical procedures
zur Routine werden*	to become routine
die Schlüssellochchirurgie/minimal invasive Chirurgie	keyhole surgery
neue Operationstechniken erproben	to try out new surgical techniques
die Genauigkeit erhöhen	to improve the accuracy

17.9 Die Gentechnologie   Genetic engineering

der DNS-Kode	DNA code
der Embryo (-nen)	embryo
die Grauzone (-n)	grey area
der Klon (-e), klonen	clone, to clone
eine Methode einsetzen	to use a technique
die Nachweismethode	detection technique
zu ... Zwecken	for ... purposes
die St~~~~~en)forschung	stem cell research

...men (*Dat pl*) neue	to give microorganisms new
...n verleihen (ei-ie-ie)	characteristics
...it menschlichen	experiments on human embryos
...Erbkrankheiten	the treatment of hereditary disease
...rschen	to map the genome

das menschliche Erbgut manipulieren	to manipulate human genetic make-up
die Unantastbarkeit/Heiligkeit des ungeborenen Lebens	the sanctity of the unborn child
eine Krankheit ausmerzen	to eradicate a disease
die Überlebensrate steigern	to raise the survival rate
die Zulassung neuer Medikamente	the licensing of new drugs
gentechnisch veränderte Nahrungsmittel	genetically modified food
Anbau, Ertrag und Haltbarkeit verbessern	to improve cultivation, yield and shelf-life

17.10 Ethische Fragen   Ethical questions

die Behandlungsmethode (-n)	method of treatment
die Designerdroge (-n)	designer drug
im Endeffekt	in the final analysis
die möglichen Folgen	the possible consequences
das Gefahrenmoment	the potential for danger
Gott spielen	to play God
harmlos	harmless
missbrauchen	to abuse
ethische/moralische Bedenken (*pl*)	moral considerations
(un)moralisch handeln	to act in a(n) (im)moral way
die Moral (*no pl*)	moral standards
eine doppelte Moral	double standards
die Moralvorstellungen (*pl*)	moral values
der Moralkodex	moral code (of society)
nützen (+*Dat*)	to benefit s.o./sth.
potenziell	potential
schädlich für (+*Acc*)	harmful to
verbieten (ie-o-o)	to forbid, ban

ein Eingriff in die Privatsphäre	invasion of privacy
lohnt es sich?	is it worth it?
wo führt das denn hin?	where will it lead us?
unvorhersehbare Folgen	unforeseeable consequences
das ist nur Zukunftsmusik!	it's just pie in the sky!
die Zukunftstechnologie	new technology
langfristig gesehen	in the long term
gegen die herrschende Moral verstoßen (ö-ie-o)	to conflict with prevailing morality
ich bin moralisch davon überzeugt, dass ...	I'm morally convinced that ...
sollten wir ... dürfen?	should we be allowed to ...?
Gewalt über sein Schicksal haben	to have power over one's destiny
wer soll die Entscheidung treffen?	whose decision is it?

auf der Seite des Fortschritts stehen (*irreg*)	to be in favour of progress
Bilanz ziehen (ie-o-o) aus (+*Dat*)	to take stock of
der Krankheit ein Ende machen	to eliminate disease
einen festen Standpunkt vertreten (i-a-e)	to take a firm stand
nicht zu rechtfertigen	indefensible, unjustifiable
moralisch nicht vertretbar	morally indefensible
von fragwürdigem Wert	of questionable value
die moralischen Aspekte der Abtreibung	the ethics of abortion
in absehbarer Zeit	in the foreseeable future
eine Behandlung, die manchem helfen wird	a treatment/cure from which many will benefit
die einzige Lösung	the only solution
es besteht die Gefahr, dass ...	there's the danger that ...
Gefahr laufen, etwas zu tun	to run the danger of doing sth.

Der Computer
http://www.bsi.de *Bundesamt für Sicherheit in der Informationstechnik*

Die Industrie
http://www.bdi-online.de/ *Bundesverband der Deutschen Industrie e.V.*
http://www.bpi.de *Bundesverband der Pharmazeutischen Industrie e.V.*
http://www.vci.de *Verband der Chemischen Industrie e.V.*

Die Forschung
http://www.bmbf.de/ *Bildung und Forschung (s. auch Kapitel 8)*
http://www.wissenschaft.de/ *Wissenschaftliche Magazin*
http://www.mpg.de/ *Max-Planck-Gesellschaft*
http://www.bmelv-forschung.de *Verbraucherschutz, Ernährung und Landwirtschaft*
http://www.weltraumforschung.de/ *die Weltraumforschung*
http://www.dlr.de/ *Deutsches Zentrum für Luft- und Raumfahrt*
http://www.gfz-potsdam.de/ *GeoForschungsZentrum Potsdam*
www.kuenstliche-intelligenz.de *Zeitschrift Künstliche Intelligenz*
http://www.ebiochip.com/ *eBiochip Systems GmbH*
http://www.transgen.de *Transparenz für Gentechnik bei Lebensmitteln*

Verschiedenes
http://www.wissenschaft-technik-ethik.de/ *Technologie und Wissenschaften*
http://www.bioethik-diskurs.de/ *Bioethik-Diskurs*
http://www.kritischebioethik.de/ *Bioethik*

18 Das Kulturleben

18.1 Die Musik   Music

die Band (-s)	band (pop)
der Chor (⁼e)	choir, chorus, choral work
der Klang (⁼e)	sound
klassische Musik	classical music
Klavier, Geige spielen	to play the piano, violin
klingen (i-a-u)	to sound
das Konzert (-e)	concerto, concert
der Musiker (-)	musician
der Musikfreund (-e)	music lover
das Stück (-e)	piece of music
üben	to practise

die alte Musik	early music
aufführen	to perform (*tr*)
auftreten* (i-a-e)	to perform (*intr*)
begleiten	to accompany
die Blechbläser (*pl*)	brass section
die Boygroup (-s)	boy band
der Chorsänger (-)	singer in choir, chorister
der Dirigent (-en)	conductor
dirigieren	to conduct
einstudieren	to rehearse
die Fahrstuhlmusik	canned music, muzak
der Flügel (-)	grand piano
die Holzbläser (*pl*)	woodwind section
der Jazz	jazz
das Kammerorchester	chamber orchestra
die Kapelle (-)	band (brass, etc.)
der Komponist (-en)	composer
komponieren	to compose, write music
der Konzertsaal (-säle)	concert hall
der Leadsänger (-)	lead singer
live singen (i-a-u), spielen	to perform live
die Melodie (-n)	tune
misstönend	discordant
das Musical (-s)	musical
die Musikbox (-en)	juke box
musizieren	to play a musical instrument

WORT FÜR WORT

die Noten (*pl*)/die Partitur (-en)	score, (sheet) music
die Oper (-n)	opera
der Rhythmus (*pl* Rhythmen)	rhythm
der Rhythm-and-Blues	rhythm and blues
die Saite (-n)	string
das Schlagzeug	percussion section
der Solist (-en)	soloist
die Streicher (*pl*)	strings section
die Symphonie (-n)	symphony
der Takt	beat
die Unterhaltungsmusik	light/easy-listening music
der Virtuose (-n)	virtuoso
die Volksmusik	folk music
in einer Band spielen	to be in a band
vom Blatt spielen	to sight-read
nach Gehör spielen	to play by ear
ins Konzert gehen	to go to a concert
die Musik sagt Teenagern zu	the music appeals to teenagers
jdn. musikalisch ausbilden	to train s.o. in music
die neuesten Musiktrends	the latest trends in music
richtig/falsch singen (i-a-u)	to sing in/out of tune
die zeitgenössische Musik	contemporary music
der Straßenmusikant (-en)	street musician, busker
auf Tournee	on tour
Übung macht den Meister	practice makes perfect

18.2 Die Kunst   Art

das Bild (-er)	picture
die Ausstellung (-en)	exhibition
darstellen	to represent
entwerfen (i-a-o)	to design
die Farbe (-n)	colour, paint
das Gemälde (-)	painting (object)
der Künstler (-)	artist
das Kunstwerk (-e)	work of art
malen/die Malerei	to paint/painting (art form)
skizzieren, die Skizze (-n)	to sketch, sketch
zeichnen	to draw

der Akt (-e)	nude figure, portrait
das Aquarell (-e)	water-colour (painting)
die Architektur/die Baukunst	architecture

architektonisch	architectural
das Atelier (-s)	studio, workshop
aufhängen (ä-i-a) *(tr)* (an der Wand)	to hang up (on the wall)
beschmieren	to daub (canvas)
der Bildhauer (-)	sculptor
das Design	Design (subject)
drucken, der Druck (-e)	to print, print (artwork)
die Galerie (-n)	gallery
die Graphik	graphic art/design
hängen (ä-i-a) *(itr)* an der Wand	to be hanging on the wall
hauen	to carve
im Hintergrund/Vordergrund	in the background/foreground
der Impressionismus	Impressionism
kitschig	trashy, posing as art
der Malstil (-e)	painting style
das Meisterwerk (-e)	masterpiece
das Modell (-e)	(artist's) model
das Ölgemälde (-)	oil painting
das Original (-e)	original
der Pinsel (-)/der Pinselstrich (-e)	brush/brush stroke
das Porträt (-s)	portrait
posieren	to pose
restaurieren	to restore
die Sammlung (-en)	collection
die Skulptur, die Bildhauerkunst	sculpture (art form)
die Skulptur (-en), die Plastik (-en)	sculpture (object)
die Statue (-n), das Standbild (-er)	statue
abstrakte Kunst	abstract art
figurative/gegenständliche Kunst	figurative art
nach dem Leben zeichnen	to draw from life
als Modell arbeiten	to model for
das kulturelle Erbe	cultural heritage
die bildenden Künste *(pl)*	fine arts

18.3 Der Film   Film

der Filmstar (-s)	film star
die Handlung	plot
die Kinokarte (-n)	cinema ticket
was läuft im Kino?	what's on at the cinema?
der Spielfilm (-e)	feature film
die Vorstellung (-en)	showing (of film)
der Zeichentrickfilm (-e)	cartoon

aktionsreich	action-packed
die Computeranimation	animatronics
das Drehbuch (¨-er)	screenplay
das Filmset (-s)	set
die Folge (-n), das Sequel (-s)	sequel
der Kinobesucher (-)	cinema-goer
das Kinocenter (-), das Multiplexkino	multi-screen cinema
der Kinorenner (-)	box-office hit
der Klassiker (-)	classic
der Knüller (-)	blockbuster
die Leinwand, die Bildwand	(cinema) screen
die Originalfassung (-en)	original version
der Regisseur (-e)	director
die Spezialeffekte (*pl*)	special effects
der Trailer (-e), die Vorschau	trailer
synchronisieren	to dub
die Zuschauer (*pl*)/das Publikum	audience

der Film ist nun überall zu sehen	the film is on general release
eine Oscar-Nominierung erhalten (ä-ie-a)	to receive an Oscar nomination
eine packende Thematik	exciting subject matter
freigegeben ab 16 Jahren	an adult film
einen Film drehen	to make a film
mit deutschen Untertiteln	with German subtitles

18.4 Das Theater   The theatre

die Aufführung (-en)	performance (of play)
die Bühne (-n)	stage
der Dramatiker (-)	playwright
die Eintrittskarte (-n)	ticket (for cinema, theatre)
die Kasse (-n)	box-office
die Pause (-n)	interval
eine Rolle spielen	to play a part
der Schauspieler (-)	actor
das Theaterstück (-e)	play

aufführen	to perform (*tr*)
auftreten*	to appear, perform (*itr*)
ausverkauft	sold out
die Beleuchtung	lighting
die Besetzung (-en)	cast
das Bühnenbild (-er)	set

durchfallen (ä-ie-a)*	to flop
der Erfolg (-e)	success
die Erstaufführung (-en)	first night
die Festspiele (pl)	festival (music, theatre, etc.)
der Flop (-s)	flop
die Generalprobe (-n)	rehearsal
der Hauptdarsteller (-)	leading actor
die Inszenierung (-en)	production
die Komödie (-n)	comedy
die Kostüme (pl)	costumes, wardrobe
die Kulissen (pl)	wings
das Laientheater	amateur dramatics
Regie führen bei (+Dat)	to direct
das Repertoiretheater	repertory theatre
der Spielplan	programme (for season)
das Programm (-e)	programme (for performance)
die Tragödie (-n)	tragedy
gegeben werden*	to be on, showing
heute wird „Faust" gegeben	today 'Faust' is on
jdm. Beifall klatschen	to applaud s.o.
wir haben ein Theaterabonnement	we have a season ticket for the theatre
die Hauptrolle spielen	to play the leading role
seine Darstellung des Hamlet(s)	his performance of Hamlet

18.5 Die Literatur — Literature

beschreiben (ei-ie-ie)	to describe
die Biografie (-n)	biography
ein Buch über (+Acc)	a book about …
darstellen	to portray
erzählen/die Erzählung (-en)	to recount, tell/short story
das Gedicht (-e)	poem
handeln von (+Dat)/die Handlung (-en)	to be about/plot
das Kapitel (-)	chapter
der Leser (-)	reader
die Phantasie	imagination
der Reißer, der Thriller	thriller
der Roman (-e)	novel
das Sachbuch (-̈er)	non-fiction

der Absatz (-̈e)	paragraph
der Ausgang	ending, dénouement
der Ausschnitt (-e)	extract
die Bedeutung (-en)	meaning

belesen	well-read
die Belletristik	fiction and poetry
der Bildungsroman (-e)	novel about the development of a character
der Bücherwurm (-̈er) ⎫ die Leseratte (-n) ⎭	bookworm
der Charakter (-)	character (personality)
die Gestalt (-en), die Figur (-en)	character (person, figure)
die Charakterisierung	characterisation
die Eigenschaft (-en)	characteristic
darstellen/schildern	to portray
der Dialog (-e)	dialogue
die Dichtung	literature, writing, poetry
der Dichter (-)	poet
das Drama	drama
sich entfalten	to unfold (*itr*)
entfalten	to unfold (*tr*)
entwickeln	to develop (*tr*)
erfunden	imaginary
der Erzähler (-)	narrator
die Frauenliteratur	books by women
die Gattung (-en)	genre
die Gruselgeschichte (-n)	horror story
die Nebenhandlung (-en)	sub-plot
das Happy End	happy end
die Hauptfigur (-en)	main character
der Held (-en)	hero
die Idee (-n)	idea
die Jugendliteratur	literature for young people
der Liebesroman (-e)	romantic novel
der Klappentext	blurb
das Meisterwerk (-e)	masterpiece
das Nachschlagewerk (-e)	reference book
die Novelle (-n)	novella
die Poesie	poetry
die Prosa	prose
die Sammlung (-en)	collection
schließlich	in the end
der Schriftsteller (-)	writer
das Taschenbuch (-̈er)	paperback
übersetzen	to translate
das Werk (-e)/gesammelte Werke (*pl*)	work/complete works
verarbeiten	to deal with (subject)
der Verlag (-e)	publisher
veröffentlichen	to publish
der Vorgang (-̈e)	event
die Zeile (-n)	line

es dreht sich um … (+Acc)	it concerns, is about …
es setzt sich kritisch mit … auseinander (+Dat)	it takes a critical look at …
es erschien bei (+Dat) …	it was published by …
neu erschienen	recently published
die gebundene Ausgabe	hardback edition
eine Erzählung in der Ich-/Er-Form	a story in the first/third person
der allwissende Erzähler	the omniscient narrator
es spielt in … (+Dat)	it is set in …
der Schauplatz der Erzählung	the scene of the story
menschliche Beziehungen (pl)	human relationships
sein Verhältnis zu seiner Frau	his relationship with his wife
sich (Dat) etw. vorstellen	to imagine sth.
sich mit einer Figur identifizieren	to identify with a character
die Trümmerliteratur	literature of the immediate post-war years
ein starkes gesellschaftliches Engagement	a strong social conscience
eine moralisch fundierte Sozialkritik	social criticism with a basis in morality
die Schattenseiten (pl) des Wirtschaftswunders	the downside to the economic miracle
es artikuliert sich in … (+Dat)	it is expressed in …
zum Thema werden	to become an issue
die Nöte und Sorgen der kleinen Leute	the problems and worries of ordinary people
das menschliche Scheitern	human failure
ich konnte das Buch einfach nicht aus der Hand legen	I just couldn't put the book down

18.6 Kultur besprechen   Discussing culture

der Aufbau	form, structure
beschreiben (ei-ie-ie)	to describe
die Eigenschaft (-en)	characteristic
enttäuschend	disappointing
erklären	to explain
ernsthaft	serious
humorvoll, heiter	humorous
lebendig	vivid
spannend	exciting
der Stil (-e)	style
das Thema (pl Themen)	subject
unterhaltsam	entertaining
unverständlich	incomprehensible
jdm. zusagen	to appeal to s.o.

analysieren	to analyse
ausdrücken	to express
berühren	to touch on
der Bezugspunkt (-e)	point of reference
der Höhepunkt (-e)	climax
der Kommentar (-e)	commentary
die Kritik (-en)	critique, criticism
kritisieren	to criticize
kultiviert	cultured (person)
die Lehre (-n)	moral point
der Materialismus	materialism
das Misstrauen gegen ... (+Acc)	mistrust of ...
das Motiv (-e)	subject
auf etw. (+Acc) reagieren	to react to sth.
schätzen	to appreciate (art, music)
sinnlos	meaningless
etw. thematisieren	to take sth. as a central theme
thematisch	as regards subject matter
das Unbehagen an ... (+Dat)	unease, disquiet at ...
vergleichen (ei-i-i)	to compare
vermitteln	to convey
das Zitat (-e)	quotation
zitieren	to quote
die Zusammenfassung	summary

etw. in Frage stellen	to question sth.
was können wir daraus entnehmen?	what can we draw/infer from this?
es lässt an (+Acc) ... denken	it suggests, evokes ...
eine Reflexion über ... (+Acc)	a reflection on ...
eine kritische Einstellung zu ... (+Dat)	a critical attitude to ...
ein zentrales Thema	a central theme
die künstlerische Freiheit beeinträchtigen	to restrict artistic freedom
es fand bei den Kritikern wenig Lob	it met with little praise from the critics

18.7 Positives   Positive points

beachtlich	relevant, excellent
die Einfühlung in (+Acc)	empathy with
ergreifend, rührend	moving
fesselnd	gripping
gefühlstief	intense
gefühlvoll	sensitive
genial	inspired

glanzvoll	sparkling
glaubwürdig	believable
humorvoll, heiter	humorous
ideenreich/der Ideenreichtum	imaginative/inventiveness
lebensnah	true to life
leicht verständlich	easily understood
liebevoll	affectionate
optimistisch	optimistic
sehr lesenswert	well worth reading
stimmungsvoll	full of atmosphere
überzeugend	convincing
unterhaltsam, kurzweilig	entertaining
warmherzig	warm-hearted
wirkungsvoll	effective
witzig	witty
zeitlos	timeless
zutreffend	accurate
wir fühlen uns in seine Lage hineinversetzt	we imagine ourselves in his position
einer der bedeutendsten Romane	one of the most significant novels
konsequent durchdacht	well thought out

18.8 Negatives   Negative points

banal	banal
belanglos	trivial
dürftig	insubstantial
das Klischee (-s)	cliché
voller Klischees	full of clichés
klischeehaft	stereotyped
mittelmäßig	mediocre
monoton	repetitive
plump	crude, obvious
schwerfällig	clumsy
schwer zu lesen	unreadable
simpel	simplistic
skurril	scurrilous
trist	drab
trocken	dry, uninspired
unglaubwürdig	unbelievable
unlogisch	illogical
unwahrscheinlich	improbable, unlikely
vage	vague
verwickelt/kompliziert	involved, convoluted
weit ausholend/weitschweifig	long-winded
zusammenhanglos	disjointed

18.9 Neutrales — Neutral points

anspruchsvoll	demanding, highbrow
anspruchslos	undemanding, lowbrow
aufwühlend	disturbing
ausführlich	detailed
brutal	violent
didaktisch	didactic, with a message
idealistisch	idealistic
ironisch	ironic
kompromisslos	uncompromising
kühl, distanziert	detached, impersonal
nostalgisch	nostalgic
pessimistisch	pessimistic
präzis	precise
realistisch	realistic
rührselig/sentimental	sentimental
umstritten	controversial
verzweifelt	despairing
zusammenschließen (ie-o-o)	to combine, bring together
es stellt hohe Ansprüche an den Leser	it makes great demands on the reader
wir bekommen dadurch einen Einblick in ... (+Acc)	it gives us an insight into ...

Die Musik

http://www.musikrat.de/ *Deutscher Musikrat*
http://www.viva.tv/ *VIVA – Musiksender*
http://www.sound.de/ *Deutschlands großes Online-Musikmagazin*
http://www.hithaus.de *deutsche Popmusik*

Die Kunst

http://www.kunstportal-deutschland.de/ *Kunstportal Deutschland*

Das Theater

http://www.buehnenverein.de/ *Theater und Orchester*
http://www.theaterheute.de/ *Fachmagazin der Theaterwelt*

Die Literatur

http://www.jugendliteratur.org/ *Arbeitskreis für Jugendliteratur e.V.*
http://www.stiftunglesen.de *Ideenwerkstatt*
http://www.die-leselust.de/ *Literatur und das Lesen*
http://www.dtv.de/ *Deutscher Taschenbuch Verlag*
http://www.buchreport.de/ *Buchreport*
www.buchmarkt.de *Magazin der Buchbranche*
http://gutenberg.spiegel.de *Deutsche Literatur online*

Verschiedenes

http://www.kulturleben.at/ *Bildung, Wissenschaft und Kultur (Österreich)*
http://www.coupe-theater.kultur-netz.de/ *Kultur-Netz*
http://www.bmbwk.gv.at/ *Bundesministerium für Bildung, Wissenschaft und Kultur (Österreich)*
www.deutsche-kultur-international.de *Bundesministerium des Innern*
http://www.kulturundsprache.at/ *Kultur und Sprache*
http://www.kulturportal-deutschland.de *Kulturportal Deutschland*
http://www.filmportal.de/ *Projekt des Deutschen Filminstituts – DIF e.V.*
www.museen.de *das Museumsportal*

19 Welches Wort soll ich wählen?

Some English words have more than one German equivalent.

after

nach (+*Dat*) (*preposition*)	nach der Pause …
nachdem (*conjunction*)	Nachdem der Film zu Ende war, …
nachher (*adverb*)	… und nachher ging er ins Café

to appear, seem, look (*see also: look*)

aussehen (=*have the appearance of*)	Er sieht krank aus.
scheinen (=*seem*)	Sie scheint ihn zu kennen.
erscheinen* (=*appear in view*)	Er ist in der Tür erschienen.
auftauchen* (=*appear after absence*)	Gestern tauchte er bei uns auf.

to ask

fragen (nach +*Dat*) (=*to ask about*)	Ich fragte ihn nach seiner Mutter.
eine Frage stellen (=*ask a question*)	Er stellt eine Frage.
bitten (um +*Acc*) (=*to ask for sth.*)	Der Lehrer bittet um Ruhe.

before

vor (+*Dat*) (*preposition*)	vor dem Film …
bevor (*conjunction*)	Bevor der Film angefangen hat, …
zuvor (*adverb*)	ein paar Tage zuvor

to care, be careful

vorsichtig (=*cautious*)	Bei Schnee vorsichtig fahren!
sorgfältig (=*painstaking*)	Er lernt alles sorgfältig.
sorgen für (+*Acc*) (=*look after, provide for*)	Wir sorgen für unsere Kinder.
es ist mir egal (=*'I don't care'*)	Es ist mir egal, ob …

to catch

fangen (=*to trap, catch, hold*)	einen Fisch/Ball fangen
erreichen (=*just catch e.g. a train*)	Erreichst du den Zug noch?

to change

ändern (*general*)	Ich habe meinen Plan geändert.
verändern (*appearance or nature*)	Sie wollte die Welt verändern.
wechseln (=*change*)	Ich meine Euros in Pfund wechsele.
umschlagen (*weather, mood*)	Seine Stimmung schlug in Aggression um.
umsteigen (*trains*)	Nach Bonn muss man in Köln umsteigen.

to decide

beschließen (*general*)	Ich beschloss ein Auto zu kaufen.
sich entscheiden (*between alternatives*)	Ich entschied mich für einen VW.
sich entschließen (*=to resolve*)	Ich entschloss mich Musiker zu werden.

different

andere (*=different to the one mentioned before*)	Mein anderer Bruder ist etwas jünger
unterschiedlich (*=varying*)	Die Wirkung ist unterschiedlich.
verschieden (*=different to one another*)	Mein Bruder und ich sind ganz verschieden.

to enjoy

(jdm.) gefallen (*=to be pleased with*)	Diese Musik gefällt mir sehr!
sich amüsieren (*=have a good time*)	Amüsiert euch gut!
Spaß an etw. (*+Dat*) haben (*=get pleasure from*)	Er hat Spaß an seinem Oldtimer.
Spaß machen (*=be fun*)	Der Abend hat uns Spaß gemacht.
genießen (*=to savour*)	einen guten Wein genießen

to feel

fühlen/empfinden (*=to feel/sense*)	Furcht/Hunger empfinden
sich fühlen (*=to feel +adverb*)	Ich fühle mich krank/unglücklich.

to get *Think of a synonym; a few of the many possibilities are:*

werden* (*=become*)	Ich werde alt.
haben (*=own*)	Sie hat ihr erstes Auto.
bekommen (*=receive*)	Ich bekam heute einen Brief.
sich (*+Dat*) etw. anschaffen/besorgen (*=buy, obtain*)	Ich muss mir einen Computer anschaffen/besorgen.
verdienen (*=earn*)	Sie verdient ein gutes Gehalt.

to know

kennen (*=be familiar with*)	jdn./eine Stadt kennen
wissen (*=by learning/experience*)	Weißt du die Lösung?

to learn

lernen (*by study*)	Sie lernt Italienisch.
erfahren (*=find out*)	Ich erfuhr die Wahrheit.

to leave

(liegen) lassen (*=leave [behind]*)	Ich ließ alles zu Hause (liegen).
verlassen (*=quit*)	Ich verlasse das Haus um 8.
abfahren* (*=set off*)	Wir fahren um 8 ab.
überlassen (*=let s.o. see to*)	Überlass es mir!

to look (*see also: appear*)

etw. ansehen (=*look at*)	Sie sah sein Foto liebevoll an.
sich (+*Dat*) etw. ansehen (=*have a look at*)	Ich will mir die Welt ansehen.
sehen auf (=*glance at*)	Ich sah auf meine Uhr.

number

die Nummer (*of house, phone*)	die Nummer meines Hauses
die Zahl (*mathematical*)	ein gutes Gedächtnis für Zahlen
die Anzahl (*indefinite*)	eine große Anzahl von Problemen

only

erst (=*not before +time*)	Ich kann erst um 8 kommen.
nur (=*no more than +quantity*)	Ich habe nur wenig Zeit.
einzige (*adj.*) (=*single*)	Er war der Einzige, der da war.

people

die Leute (*pl*) (=*group of people*)	Sie sind sehr nette Leute.
die Menschen (*pl*) (=*people in general*)	Alle Menschen müssen sterben.
die Personen (*pl*) (=*individuals*)	eine Familie aus 6 Personen
das Volk (=*nation*)	das deutsche Volk
viele (=*many people*)	Viele sind der Meinung, dass ...

to put

legen (=*lying down*)	Er legte das Buch auf den Tisch.
stellen (=*standing*)	Stell die Flasche auf den Tisch!
stecken (=*put into*)	Er steckt die Hand in die Tasche.
tun (*in general – colloquial*)	Tu die Tassen in den Schrank!

same

gleich (=*alike, equal*)	Wir tragen die gleiche Hose.
(der)selbe (=*selfsame*)	Wir haben dieselbe Mutter.

to stop

halten (*itr*) (=*halt*)	Der Bus hält hier.
anhalten (*tr/itr*) (*temporary, unexpected*)	Plötzlich hielt er das Auto an.
aufhalten (*tr*) (=*delay, hinder*)	Der Streik hält den Brief auf.
aufhören (*itr*) (=*stop doing sth.*)	Es hörte auf zu regnen.

to stay

bleiben (=*remain in one place/condition*)	Er blieb den ganzen Tag bei uns.
wohnen/sich aufhalten (=*be based temporarily*)	Er hält sich im Hotel auf.
verbringen (=*spend time*)	Ich verbringe 3 Tage in den USA.
übernachten (=*stay the night*)	Du kannst bei uns übernachten.

to take

nehmen (=*pick up, use*)	Nimm den Zug/dieses Buch!
bringen (*someone somewhere*)	Ich bringe dich zum Bahnhof.
dauern (*time*)	Die Reise hat 2 Stunden gedauert.

there is/are (*Much less used in German than English. Avoid where possible.*)

es gibt (*general*)	Es gibt einen Gott. (Gott existiert.)
es ist/sind (*specific time, place*)	Es ist ein Mann im Auto. (Ein Mann sitzt ...)

thing

die Sache (-n) (=*possession*)	Hast du deine Sachen mit?
(=*affair, subject*)	Sport ist nicht meine Sache.
das Ding (*object*)	Was ist das für ein Ding?
(*pl =serious matters*)	Diese Dinge gehen nur mich an.
+ *the adjective + thing*	Das Beste/Schlimmste ist, ...
überhaupt nichts	not a thing
seinen eigenen Weg gehen	to do one's own thing

to think

denken an (=*have in mind*)	Woran denkst du?
denken/halten von (=*have an opinion on*)	Was hältst du von ihm?
halten für (=*consider to be*)	Ich halte es für das Beste, wenn ...
nachdenken über (=*weigh up*)	Ich muss darüber nachdenken, ob ...
meinen (=*give an opinion*)	Ich meine, es wäre besser, wenn ...

time

die Zeit (-en) (*period*)	Ich habe keine Zeit dazu.
das Mal (-e) (*occasion*)	Sie ist zum ersten Mal hier.
jdm. Spaß machen (*a good time*)	Es hat mir Spaß gemacht!

to (+*place*)

nach (+*town, country*)	Wir fahren nach Kiel/nach Irland.
zu (*to a destination*)	Ich fahre zur Schule.
in (*implies 'into'*)	Ich gehe in die Stadt/ins Kino/ ins Konzert/in die Schule.

to try

versuchen (=*attempt*)	Ich versuchte ihm zu helfen.
probieren (=*sample*)	Probieren Sie diesen Wein!
an-/ausprobieren (=*try on/out*)	Hast du diese Methode ausprobiert?

to use

benutzen, verwenden (=*to utilise*)	Ich benutze immer ein Wörterbuch.
gebrauchen (=*utilise sth. one has*)	Er gebraucht einen Kuli.
nutzen (=*to exploit, positively*)	Sie nutzt jede Chance.
ausnutzen (=*to exploit, negatively*)	Er nutzt ihre Gutmütigkeit aus.
anwenden (=*to apply*)	Sie hat diese Methode angewandt.
verbrauchen (=*to consume*)	Dieses Auto verbraucht viel Benzin.

to work

arbeiten (=*labour*)	Sie hat sich nach oben gearbeitet.
funktionieren, gehen (=*function*)	Meine Uhr geht nicht.
klappen (=*to work out*) (*inf*)	Ich hoffe, dass es klappt.
ausdenken (*to work out scheme*)	Ich muss mir einen Plan ausdenken.